How To Save Inheritance Tax

How To Save Inheritance Tax

Understand how inheritance tax works – and pass on more of your hard-earned wealth to those you love

Gordon Bowley LLB

howtobooks

Published by How To Books Ltd,
Spring Hill House, Spring Hill Road,
Begbroke, Oxford OX5 1RX. United Kingdom.
Tel: (01865) 375794. Fax: (01865) 379162.
info@howtobooks.co.uk
www.howtobooks.co.uk

How To Books greatly reduce the carbon footprint of their books by sourcing their typesetting and
printing in the UK

British Library Cataloguing in Publication Data
A catalogue record for this book is available from the British Library

ISBN 978 1 84528 260 8

Produced for How To Books by Deer Park Productions, Tavistock, Devon
Typeset by PDQ Typesetting, Newcastle-under-Lyme, Staffs.
Printed and bound in Great Britain by Bell & Bain Ltd, Glasgow

NOTE: The material contained in this book is set out in good faith for general guidance and no liability
can be accepted for loss or expense incurred as a result of relying in particular circumstances on
statements made in the book. The law and regulations are complex and liable to change, and readers
should check the current position with the relevant authorities before making personal arrangements.

To my wife Margaret and my son John
as a token of my appreciation of their kindness and devotion to me.

Contents

Preface

There are some events that are so terrible that we choose to close our eyes to them and to enter into a state of denial. Although we know in our hearts that it is not true, we choose to think that they will not happen to us and yet they inevitably do. Our own deaths are such events. Although the desire to preserve our hard-earned wealth and to pass as much of it as we can to our families and friends when we can no longer use it is basic and one of the strongest of human desires, we tend to put off making arrangements to do so and avoid tax planning. And yet, if we can summon up the courage to face up to our deaths and inheritance tax, it can be a great comfort to know that there are steps we can take to ensure that more of our hard-earned cash is passed on to those we care for and who care for us and less of it will be used to replenish governmental coffers.

Have you that courage? If so this book will help you take those steps.

Inheritance tax is an intensely technical and increasingly important and complex subject, but this book is intended to give non-lawyers a more than basic understanding of the tax and to point them on the way to understanding how they can order their financial affairs and arrange their wealth in such a way as to pass on as much of it as they can comfortably afford to do so to those they care for, rather than leaving it for the state to dissipate. I do not claim that this book will enable the reader to carry complex schemes to fruition personally (no one who has not devoted many years to the study of the specialist subject of tax can hope to do that), but I hope that this book will enable you to see what your particular situation is and where and how it might be considerably improved. It will enable you to talk with your advisers intelligently and to judge their worth. It should also prove to be of value to law and accountancy students approaching the subject for the first time.

When writing the book I tried to avoid the use of jargon and technical terms whenever possible, but when dealing with a technical subject, for reasons of readability and accuracy, it is impossible to avoid technical terms and terms of art entirely and accordingly a glossary has been included to explain them, as far as possible, in simple, everyday language.

Throughout the book, for simplicity's sake and not for any reasons of gender prejudice, I have assumed that the usual case of the male of the species predeceasing the female will occur and 'he' should be read as 'she' or 'they' where the context and circumstances so require.

The book deals with the law applicable to the United Kingdom other than the Channel Islands and the Isle of Man where revenue law differs. Moreover, law, practice and personal circumstances change frequently and while every effort has been made to ensure that the contents of the book are accurate and up to date, no responsibility is accepted for any loss resulting from acting or failure to act as a result of it and the book is sold and bought on that basis. In particular, changes that might be made to the inheritance tax nil-rate exemption band or tax rates by future Finance Acts should be borne in mind.

Crown copyright is acknowledged in respect of all statutory and governmental material quoted or referred to in the text.

Gordon Bowley

An Explanation of the Nature of Inheritance Tax and How it Works

WHAT IS THE NATURE OF INHERITANCE TAX?

Inheritance tax is, in essence, a tax on giving and on giving in a very wide sense of the word. The tax applies to gifts which are made during the life of the taxpayer, to gifts made by the taxpayer's will at the moment of his death and to gifts which the state's laws of intestacy deem that he would have made at that instant had indolence, incompetence, forgetfulness, procrastination or indeed sheer cussedness not caused him to die without a valid will. As far as the government and the Inland Revenue are concerned, it seems that the distinction between tax avoidance (arranging one's affairs so as to incur as little tax as possible) and tax evasion (dodging the tax which is incurred and legally due) is becoming increasingly blurred and disappearing into the mists. The state is determined and struggles valiantly to ensure that it shall have its tax and often the taxpayer's death is the first occasion upon which he pays tax at the highest rate. The state will have its pound of flesh, even though it might be tardy in taking it.

If the state is not to get his bones along with a kilo of his flesh, the taxpayer needs to have a basic understanding of how the tax works, how it is calculated and how it applies to his own particular circumstances.

IN WHAT CIRCUMSTANCES DOES A LIABILITY TO THE TAX ARISE AND WHAT PROPERTY INCURS LIABILITY TO THE TAX?

The law of inheritance tax is based upon the Inheritance Tax Act 1984 as subsequently amended. In broad terms the tax becomes payable whenever a person's wealth is reduced, that is to say there is a **transfer of value,** as the result of a gratuitous transfer of property (i.e. the making of a gift) or a failure to act, unless the transfer or the failure is within one of the exceptions specified by the Act or the amendments (when it is known as an '**exempt disposition**'). A transfer is also exempt if the property in respect of which the transfer takes place is '**excluded property**', which is defined in the Act and its amendments, or if it is a gift which is exempted from the tax by the Act. The tax payable is less if the inheritance tax '**reliefs**' specified in the Act notionally reduce either the value of the property or the tax itself.

In slightly greater detail and using more technical terms, if a taxpayer has his **domicile in the United Kingdom** or is deemed to have it there, inheritance tax is charged whenever there is any **gratuitous transfer of value** (other than an **exempt disposition** or **exempt gift**) in respect of any of his assets in whatever country they may be, unless it is a transfer of **excluded property** and whether the transfer takes place during the taxpayer's lifetime or on his death. The tax is calculated by reference to the value transferred.

If the taxpayer's domicile or deemed domicile is outside the United Kingdom, the tax only applies to those of his assets (other than excluded property) that are situated in the United Kingdom.

The fundamental concepts to keep in mind when considering liability for inheritance tax are those set out in **bold type** above. The meanings of 'domicile' and 'deemed domicile' are explained below, transfer of value is explained on pages 6–7, exempt dispositions are enumerated on pages 7–9, the exempt gifts are set out on pages 12–15 and a list of excluded property is set out on pages 9–10.

The questions to be asked are:

♦ Is the taxpayer domiciled or deemed to be domiciled in the United Kingdom?

♦ Has there been a gratuitous transfer of value? (see page 6).

♦ If so 'Was the transfer an exempt disposition?' (see page 7).

♦ If the transfer was not an exempt disposition, 'Are the assets which were transferred excluded property (see pages 9–10) or was the gift an exempt gift? (See pages 12–15).

Ascertaining domicile

Domicile must not be confused with residence. A person has his tax residence in the state where he spends most of his time or has accommodation so that he can spend most of his time there. Residence is of little or no importance as far as inheritance tax is concerned. The concept of domicile is extremely important when considering liability for inheritance tax. Broadly speaking and subject to the concept of deemed domicile, a person has his domicile in the state which he considers to be his permanent home, even though he might have no legal right to live there.

Domicile of origin

At birth a person has the same domicile as his mother if he is illegitimate or his father is dead, otherwise the domicile of the father. This is known as domicile of origin.

Domicile of choice

A person who is legally mentally capable and over the age of 16 can exchange a domicile of origin for what is known as a domicile of choice by abandoning ties with the state in which he has his domicile of origin and moving to live in the other state *with the intention of living there indefinitely or making it his permanent home.* This is so even if he is an illegal immigrant and has no legal right to be in that other state.

To acquire a domicile of choice in a state one must be both resident there and have the intention of residing in the state either indefinitely or permanently; to lose a domicile of choice one must both cease to reside in the state and change one's intention to reside there indefinitely or permanently. If a domicile of choice or dependency is lost and no new domicile of choice is acquired, the domicile of origin is reacquired.

A new domicile of choice can be acquired as frequently as is desired, but it is only possible to have one domicile at any given time and the burden of proving a change of domicile lies upon the person who asserts that it has taken place . The standard of proof required is that it must be proved on a balance of probabilities that the change of domicile has taken place; i.e. it is not necessary to prove without any reasonable doubt that the change has taken place but only that it is more likely than not that it has taken place. It should be noted that the decisions of Her Majesty's

Inland Revenue and Customs (henceforth referred to as 'the Revenue') on the question are not binding on the courts.

Domicile of dependency

Those who are mentally incapable or under the age of 16 have the domicile of the person upon whom they are dependent and their domicile will follow any change in that person's domicile. This is known as a domicile of dependency. A woman who married before 1 January 1974 acquired her husband's domicile by virtue of the marriage, but after that date she can change it and her domicile is no longer dependent upon her husband.

Deemed domicile

There are exceptions to the above rules for inheritance tax purposes, in that for those purposes:

- people are deemed to retain their domicile in the relevant part of the United Kingdom for three years after leaving it

- those who have been resident in any part of the United Kingdom are deemed to be domiciled here if they have been resident here for at least 17 or more of the 20 preceding *tax* years.

People who are deemed to be domiciled in the United Kingdom for inheritance tax purposes might be able to claim a non-United Kingdom domicile for capital gains tax and income tax purposes.

The United Kingdom for the purpose of inheritance tax includes England, Wales, Scotland and Northern Ireland but does not include the Channel Islands or the Isle of Man.

The word 'state' is used in connection with domicile rather than 'country' because domicile is defined not by national boundaries but by places that have their own independent system of law.

Transfers of value

A transfer of value is defined in the Inheritance Tax Act 1984 (Section 3) as 'a disposition made by a person ... as a result of which the value of his estate immediately after the disposition is less than it would be but for the disposition; and the amount by which it is less is the "value transferred" by the transfer'. Therefore calculation of inheritance tax is based upon the reduction the transaction causes to the wealth of the giver and not the increase in the recipient's wealth, which is not always the same, and will never be the same if the value of an asset is greater than the value of its separate parts and only part is transferred. Consider the example of a pair of candlesticks. A pair is worth more than two single ones and the loss suffered by giving one away and retaining the other is greater than the gain obtained by receiving one. Similarly, in the case of a gift of shares by a shareholder who has a controlling interest in a company, a gift of a number of shares which reduces the giver's shareholding so that it is no longer a controlling interest in the company is a transfer of greater value than a gift of the same number of shares by any other shareholder and the benefit to a recipient who does not obtain control of the company by the gift is less than the loss to the giver.

A disposition includes not only a positive act, but also failure to exercise a right, if the failure was deliberate and increases the value of another person's assets. For example:

- the failure by a landlord to exercise a right given by the lease to review and increase rent

- a failure to attempt to collect a debt

- failure to use a power given by a will or settlement to appoint property to oneself.

Taxable and non-taxable dispositions

Some transactions which cause a reduction in the taxpayer's wealth are declared by the Act not to be transfers of value and are therefore not **taxable** dispositions and are exempt.

- A disposition which 'is not intended . . . to confer any gratuitous benefit' **and** which is either entered into at arm's length between 'persons not connected with each other' or which is 'such as might be expected to be' entered into 'at arms [*sic*] length between persons not connected with each other' is not taxable (section 10 of the Inheritance Tax Act 1984). Persons connected with each other for this purpose are, roughly speaking, the taxpayer's family including his spouse or civil partner, his ancestors, lineal descendants, brothers and sisters, uncles and aunts, nephews and nieces, the spouse or civil partner of the above family members and the relatives in the same categories of the taxpayer's spouse or civil partner. Except in respect of commercial transactions relating to the partnership assets, the taxpayer's business partner and the partner's spouse or registered civil partner are also considered to be connected to him. This section prevents normal commercial transactions which in the event prove to have been loss-making from the taxpayer's point of view from being caught by inheritance tax.

EXAMPLE

An example might assist. Suppose Mr A buys a florist's shop from Mrs B, to whom he pays what turns out to be a good price and who is unconnected with him, because he thinks that he can run it more profitably, but he is mistaken and the venture fails. The overpriced purchase will not be a disposition by Mr A for inheritance tax purposes because although the price transferred value from his estate to hers, he had no gratuitous intent and she was not a 'connected person'. If he had bought it from his nephew, the transaction would not be a taxable disposal because although it was a transaction with a connected person it was made on the same terms as it would have been made upon if negotiated at arm's length between persons not connected with each other and he did not intend to confer any gratuitous benefit. If he had bought the shop as a gift for his daughter-in-law the transfer to the daughter-in-law would have been a taxable disposal by Mr A because of the gratuitous element in favour of the daughter-in-law. If he had bought the shop with a view to changing the use to that of a newsagents to assist a friend who ran a competing florist's nearby by removing the competition, the transaction would have been a taxable disposal because he would be intending to confer a gratuitous benefit on his friend, even though his friend was not a party to the transaction.

◆ Transfers made during the taxpayer's life in favour of a spouse, registered civil partner or a child of the taxpayer or child of his spouse or registered civil partner, for the purpose of family maintenance. This exemption applies not only during the subsistence of the relationship but also in respect of arrangements made on the annulment or dissolution of the relationship, e.g. on divorce, and upon the variation of such arrangements. It also applies to transfers for the reasonable maintenance of a dependant relative. In the case of a child it only applies to transfers of value for the maintenance, education or training of the child until the year in which the child attains the age of 18 or until he ceases to undergo full-time education or training, if later.

♦ The grant of an agricultural tenancy for full consideration payable in money or money's worth. Consideration in law is the price of a legal bargain or agreement; for example, in the grant of a tenancy it might be a lump sum or a rent or both.

There are also a few other dispositions connected with companies and employment which are declared not to be taxable, such as waiver of dividends in the 12-month period before the right to the dividends arises.

Excluded property, i.e. property which is never liable to incur inheritance tax

The following are excluded property:

♦ Savings Certificates and Premium Bonds owned by people who are domiciled in the Channel Islands or the Isle of Man.

♦ Certain British government stock owned by those living abroad.

♦ Certain overseas pensions and lump sums payable on death.

♦ Emoluments and tangible movable property which is owned by visiting armed forces.

♦ Property of service people who die as a result of active military service.

♦ By concession, decorations awarded for valour or gallantry. (not necessarily in a military context), which have never been transferred in return for money or money's worth. The decoration need not have remained in the same family and need not have been a medal but could be a sword or silverware, for example.

♦ Property situated outside the United Kingdom which belongs to a person who is domiciled outside the United Kingdom.

♦ Foreign-currency bank accounts with most banks in the United Kingdom that are held by people who are of foreign domicile and not resident or ordinarily resident in the United Kingdom.

♦ Most reversionary interests, i.e. most presently owned rights to property upon the death of someone who is currently entitled to the property during their lifetime under a trust. As an example consider the following: A by his will left his house on trust for B during B's life and after B's death for C. After A's death B would have a life interest in the house and be known as the tenant for life and C would have a reversionary interest in the house and be known as the remainderman. Reversionary interests are excluded property unless they are rights to which the person who set up the trust or his spouse or civil partner is or has been entitled or they have been acquired at any time for money or money's worth (e.g. by exchange for something which could have been sold).

Which assets incur a liability to inheritance tax (unless they are specifically exempted by legislation or are excluded property)?

The taxpayer's assets that suffer inheritance tax, unless they are assets specifically exempted by legislation or excluded property, are as follows:

1. Everything the taxpayer owns (including his share of any property he owns jointly with anyone else).

2. Everything he has given away in the last seven years of his life unless they are exempt gifts as specified on pages 12–15.

3. Every non-exempt gift he has ever made from which he has reserved a right to benefit in the last seven years.

4. Everything owned by someone else from which the taxpayer is entitled to benefit for the remainder of the taxpayer's life or for any other limited period, (called a life tenancy), e.g. the full market value of any house in which the taxpayer has the right to live rent free for the remainder of his life or the assets of any trust fund of which the taxpayer has a right to the income for the remainder of his life, if

    –   the life tenant was entitled as a disabled person under a trust for the disabled as explained in Chapter 7, or
    –   the life tenancy was created by a will or intestacy and began immediately upon the death, or
    –   the life tenancy was created by an arrangement or trust created before 22 March 2006, or
    –   the life tenancy follows immediately upon a life tenancy in existence on 6 April 2006 that ended before 6 April 2008, or
    –   the life tenant was the spouse or civil partner of a person who was a life tenant under a pre-6 April 2006 trust at that date who died on or after 6 April 2008 and the life tenant's entitlement immediately followed on that of his spouse or civil partner, or
    –   the life tenancy is the first or a subsequent life tenancy in a trust created before 22 of March 2006 which is a trust of a life policy or life policies, provided that there has been no break in the sequence of life tenancies.

1, 2 and 3 above are known as the taxpayer's free estate and 4, is known as his settled estate.

From the total of these assets it is permissible to deduct the debts and financial liabilities transferred with the assets to which they relate and if the transfer of value takes place as the result of the taxpayer's death, the amount of the taxpayer's debts and reasonable funeral and mourning expenses, but if the taxpayer is insolvent it is not permissible to deduct any deficiency in the free estate from the settled estate.

Exempt Gifts

The gifts, i.e. gratuitous transfers of value, that are exempt from inheritance tax are the following.

♦ Out-and-out gifts made by the taxpayer more than seven years prior to his death without retaining any benefit from the gift, unless the gift is made to a company or to a trust (other than a trust for the disabled). Gifts made to a company or to a trust (other than a trust for the disabled) are known as immediately chargeable gifts. With the exception of immediately chargeable gifts, gifts remain only potentially liable to inheritance tax for the seven years after they have been made and are known as PETs (potentially exempt transfers), a concept and an acronym which should be remembered because they will feature prominently in later pages. If the donor survives the making of a PET by seven years the PET is completely exempt from the tax whatever its value.

♦ Gifts of any amount to a spouse or civil partner, unless the taxpayer is domiciled in the United Kingdom but the spouse or civil partner is not, in which case the exemption is limited to £55,000.

◆ Gifts of not more than £3,000 in total made in any tax year during the life of the taxpayer. Any unused benefit from this exemption can be carried forward for one, but only one, tax year and the annual exemption for any current tax year is used up before the unused balance of the annual exemption from any previous tax year.

EXAMPLE

Suppose, therefore, that a taxpayer makes a gift of £1,000 to his son in tax year 1 and a gift of £4,000 to his daughter in year 2. In tax year 1 the £1,000 gift is exempt because it is less than the £3,000 exemption level and there is £2,000 of the exemption for year 1 that can be carried forward to tax year 2. In tax year 2 the benefit of the £2,000 unused exemption from year 1 is available, together with the £3,000 annual exemption for year 2, to be set against the gift of £4,000 made to the daughter in year 2, with the result that that gift is also completely exempt, but the rule is that the excess of £2,000 from year 1 is to be used up after the £3,000 annual exemption for current year 2 has been applied and accordingly only £1,000 of the excess from year 1 is used in year 2. Because it can only be carried forward for one year, £1,000 of the £2,000 unused from the exemption in year 1 is wasted and cannot be used against any gift of over £3,000 made in tax year 3. ◼

If the total value of gifts which are not covered by any other exemption in any tax year exceeds this annual exemption and any useable balance from any previous tax year, the excess is taxable.

◆ Gifts made during the taxpayer's lifetime which are made as part of the normal expenditure of the taxpayer out of his income and not from capital and which do not reduce his standard of living. Normal expenditure is expenditure which is in accordance with a settled pattern of the donor's expenditure and that pattern may be proved either by showing that the taxpayer has made such payments regularly in the past or that he has taken a decision to make them in the future, for example, by entering into a covenant to do so. There is no minimum period during which the payments must be made as long as the period is more than nominal and a single payment will be sufficient if there is sufficient evidence to show an intention to continue them.

♦ Wedding gifts made before the ceremony during the taxpayer's lifetime, up to £5,000 to his child, up to £2,500 to his grandchild and up to £1,000 in the case of anyone else.

♦ Gifts made in the taxpayer's lifetime for the maintenance of a spouse, ex-spouse, civil-partner, ex-civil partner, dependant relatives and dependant children who are under the age of 18 or are in full-time education.

♦ Gifts to registered charities for charitable purposes.

♦ Gifts for certain national purposes including gifts to most museums and art galleries and to political parties which have at least two sitting members of the House of Commons or which have one sitting member and whose candidates polled 150,000 votes at the last general election.

♦ Gifts of land to registered housing associations.

Gifts in any number of the above classes can be made to the same person without losing the benefit of the exemption and in addition, under what is known as the small gifts exemption, any number of gifts of up to £250 can be made in a tax year provided that no other gift has been made to the same person in the same tax year. If the sum given under the small gifts exemption exceeds £250 the benefit of the exemption is lost and the entire sum is taxable. This is in contrast to the situation in respect of the annual exemption where only the excess over the amount of the exemption is taxable and the remainder is exempt.

Married people and those with a registered civil partner should remember that each spouse and civil partner has a separate set of gift exemptions.

The percentage of the value of any gift which is not an exempt disposition or a gift of excluded property that is extracted as tax, i.e. the rate of tax charged, is dependent upon:

◆ whether the gift is deemed to have been made at the time of the taxpayer's death or whether it was made during his life and, if so, how long he survived the making of the gift

◆ who or what organisation was the recipient of the gift

◆ the type of property given.

It is therefore essential to keep full documentary evidence which shows the dates and the value of all gifts, what was given and to whom the gifts were made. If it is likely that the normal expenditure exemption will be relied upon it is also necessary to keep details of all income, income tax paid, spending, bills and other expenses for the relevant year at least.

2

Calculating Inheritance Tax

THE NIL-RATE BAND

Every tax year the government decides upon a sum below which value no inheritance tax is payable in respect of taxable transfers of value. This sum is known as the tax threshold. The rate of tax payable in respect of taxable transfers of value in the band between zero and the tax threshold is nil and accordingly the band is known as the nil-rate band. Transfers of value within the nil-rate band are not exempt transfers; they are taxable but the rate of tax charged is nil. When once the total of all taxable transfers which have been made exceeds the tax threshold, tax is charged upon the excess at the rate applicable to lifetime chargeable transfers or to chargeable transfers on death, as appropriate. The present tax threshold is £300,000 and it will be £312,000 in 2008/9 and £325,000 in 2009/10. The rate applicable to lifetime chargeable transfers in excess of the nil-rate band is 20% and the rate applicable to chargeable transfers on death in excess of the nil-rate band is 40%.

VALUING GIFTS AND TRANSFERS OF VALUE

Gifts and transfers of value are valued for inheritance tax purposes at the amount by which the estate of the person making the transfer is diminished as a result of the transfer and not by the amount by which the recipient or any other person benefits from the transfer.

HOW TO CALCULATE INHERITANCE TAX PAYABLE ON GIFTS MADE IN LIFE

To calculate the amount of inheritance tax payable on a gift made during life:

1. total all the chargeable transfers of value made by the giver within the previous seven tax years taking care to exclude any exempt gifts and gifts of excluded property

2. deduct any debts and financial liabilities which are transferred with the asset to which the debt or financial liability relates, e.g. any mortgage upon the property given if the recipient is to be responsible for discharging the mortgage debt

3. deduct the balance of the tax threshold which remains unused by previous non-exempt gifts made in the previous seven years

4. apply the full lifetime rate of tax to the resultant figure

5. if the transfer was made more than three years before death, apply taper relief to the amount of tax so ascertained (not to the value of the transfer) (taper relief is explained in Chapter 5).

HOW TO CALCULATE INHERITANCE TAX PAYABLE ON DEATH

To calculate the inheritance tax payable on a death estate, add the total of the net death estate to the total of the chargeable lifetime gifts made in the previous seven years and deduct any balance of the tax threshold which has not been used in respect of the lifetime gifts. Apply the full death tax rate to the resultant figure and then deduct the full tax payable on the lifetime gifts (calculated as above before the application of taper relief).

PERMISSIBLE DEDUCTIONS WHEN CALCULATING THE NET ESTATE ON A DEATH

The deductions that it is permissible to make from the total of the values which have been transferred by a death are:

♦ any legacies which are exempt gifts, e.g. legacies to a spouse or to a registered charity for its charitable purposes

♦ reasonable funeral and mourning expenses including the cost of a memorial

♦ any debts and liabilities existing at the date of death for which the taxpayer had received value or that were imposed by the law, e.g. outstanding income tax, but not the inheritance tax payable as the result of the death

♦ the cost of realising or administering any property which is situated outside the United Kingdom up to 50% of its value

♦ excluded property.

CALCULATING THE NIL-RATE BAND WHICH REMAINS AVAILABLE ON DEATH

Any non-exempt gift (other than a gift of excluded property) made in the seven years before a death is deducted from, and will reduce, the tax exemption threshold available to be set against the net estate at death by the value transferred by the gift, but exempt gifts (listed on pages 12–15), do not do so.

CALCULATING THE NIL-RATE BAND WHICH IS AVAILABLE WHEN MAKING AN IMMEDIATELY CHARGEABLE LIFETIME GIFT

When dealing with **immediately chargeable** lifetime gifts (gifts made during one's life to trusts, other than trusts for the benefit of disabled beneficiaries, or to companies), to calculate the value of the inheritance tax exemption threshold which is available to be set against the gift, it is necessary to deduct from the then current inheritance tax threshold figure the total value of all **immediately chargeable** gifts made by the giver in the previous seven years. If the total value of the immediately chargeable gifts made in the previous seven years and the current gift exceeds the current inheritance tax threshold, tax is payable on the excess. **Gifts other than immediately chargeable gifts** are ignored and are not deducted from the threshold figure when calculating how much of the nil-rate band remains and is available to be set off against an immediately chargeable gift, because being PETs, they are still potentially exempt and not chargeable.

Gifts are deducted from the inheritance tax threshold in the chronological order in which they are made. For example, assuming that no other non-exempt gifts have been made, if a gift of £250,000 is made to X and 13 months later a similar amount is given to Y, the donor dying one month after the second gift, the gift to X will be exempt from tax (being below the tax exemption threshold) but the gift to Y will probably suffer some tax, the amount of tax depending upon the amount of the threshold at the date of the death.

If the total value of **immediately chargeable** non-exempt gifts made in the previous seven years and the value of the immediately chargeable gift currently being made exceeds the then tax threshold, inheritance tax (at one-half of the rate then payable in respect of gifts made on death) is immediately payable on the excess. Credit is given on death for tax that has been paid on immediately chargeable gifts made in the previous seven years, but if the tax paid exceeds the tax payable on them at death the excess is not repayable.

EXAMPLE

Consider the following example. In June 1989 wealthy and generous Mr A makes a gift of £50,000 to his son and in July 1996 a gift of £10,000 to his favourite registered charity. In 1997 he makes a gift of £20,000 into a trust for his grandchildren. No inheritance tax is payable at the time of the 1989 and 1996 gifts because:

1. they are not **immediately chargeable** transfers of value
2. because they are not in total more than the tax threshold
3. in respect of the July gift to the registered charity, it is not counted because it falls within the list of exempt gifts.

When the 1997 gift is made into the trust, no tax is payable because although the gift is an immediately chargeable transfer:

1. the July gift is not to be counted because it is an exempt gift
2. the 1989 gift to the son is exempt, having been made over seven years previously and also it was not an immediately chargeable gift. Further, it is not taken into account when calculating how much of the inheritance tax exemption threshold has been used and the 1997 gift is below the unused inheritance tax threshold.

On 30 May 1998 when the exemption threshold was £223,000, Mr A makes a further transfer of £220,000 to the trust and the trustees pay the tax in respect of the transfer. The tax payable on the 1998 immediately chargeable lifetime gift to the trust is calculated by deducting from the then tax threshold of £223,000 the total of that gift and the total of all **immediately chargeable** gifts made in the previous seven years (but ignoring any other previously made gifts, including any that are not immediately chargeable transfers which were made in the previous seven years) and taxing the balance. To put it another way, tax is payable on the sum by which the value of the gift and the immediately chargeable non-exempt gifts made in the previous seven years exceeds the current tax threshold. Therefore the tax payable in 1998 is at 20% (the lifetime rate being one-half of the death rate of 40%), chargeable on £17,000, being the total of the 1997 and 1998 immediately chargeable transfers (£240,000) minus then exempt threshold of £223,000, i.e. £3,400 tax. ■

As has been previously explained and with the exception of cumulation which is explained in the following section, transfers made more than seven years before death are exempt transfers. Transfers made in the seven years immediately preceding death are potentially exempt until death occurs, unless they are immediately chargeable gifts. Transfers other than immediately chargeable transfers are not taken into account when calculating the tax payable on immediately chargeable transfers until death occurs when a revision of the tax might or might not become necessary, depending on how long has elapsed between the transfer and death. Referring back to the example given above, if Mr A had died on 9 May 2005 leaving a net estate of £300,000, the tax on the 1998 transfer to the trust would have to be revised because it was made within seven years of the death and tax would be payable at the death rate of 40% instead of at the lifetime rate of 20%. The amount of the nil-rate band used up by the 1997 gift to the trust would remain the same in this calculation but allowance would be made for the tax already paid. The tax payable in respect of the 1998 gift would therefore be £6,800 (40% of

£17,000) and after allowing for the tax paid at the time of the 1998 gift a further £3,400 would have to be paid.

The tax payable on the death estate would be calculated as follows:

Estate at death on 9 May 2005	£300,000
Add value of gifts made in the previous seven years	£220,000
	£520,000
Deduct remaining value of 2005 nil-rate band of £275,000 (£275,000 − £220,000)	£55,000
£55,000 charged at current rate of 40%:	£22,000

For the sake of comparative simplicity any available reliefs and exemptions have been ignored in the above calculations.

Cumulation

Chargeable transfers made within the seven-year period prior to a chargeable transfer are taken into account when calculating the tax on the presently made chargeable transfer, whether those chargeable transfers are immediately chargeable lifetime transfers or potentially exempt transfers which have become chargeable as a result of the transferor's death occurring within the following seven years.

3

Valuation of Assets for Inheritance Tax Purposes

HOW TO VALUE ASSETS FOR THE PURPOSE OF CALCULATING THE VALUE TRANSFERRED

Assets are valued for the purposes of inheritance tax at their open market value, that is to say at the price which would be obtained for them in a sale at arm's length to a stranger and between a willing seller and a willing buyer. Such a valuation will differ from an insurance valuation, which would be on the basis of the cost of replacing the asset new or a valuation on the basis of a forced sale. Like any other valuation, an open market valuation is a matter of opinion and conjecture unless the market has been thoroughly tested, but certain rules exist to assist the valuation and the Revenue can impose penalties if valuations are fraudulently or negligently made.

Unit trusts

Unit trusts have two prices: one at which the trust managers are prepared to sell the units and a lower price at which the trust managers are prepared to buy them back. For inheritance tax purposes unit trusts are valued at the lower of the two prices. The *Financial Times* newspaper gives the prices for the previous day.

Corporate bonds, government stock and other stocks and shares quoted on a recognised stock exchange

These securities also have a buying price and a lower selling price. The taxpayer can choose which of two figures he wishes to use.

The first figure is calculated by adding to the lower selling price at which the security last traded on the relevant day one-quarter of the difference between the selling and the buying price. The second figure is the figure which is halfway between the highest and the lowest price recorded for bargains (excluding special bargains) for the relevant day. If the stock exchange was not open for trading on the relevant day, either the previous or the next trading day may be used. For a small fee the London Stock Exchange Historic Price Service, which can be consulted on its website http://www.londonstockexchange.co.uk or in writing, will supply the final prices for the relevant day for any quoted security and, if the security was quoted ex-dividend, the dividend rate per share. The current fee can be obtained by telephoning, emailing or faxing the service. Alternatively valuations of stocks or shares for inheritance tax purposes can be obtained from most banks, stockbrokers or from www.sharedata.co.uk but they do charge for the service and it might be wise to ask for an indication of the likely fee in advance.

If a share is quoted 'ex-dividend', the dividend which has been declared must be included in the valuation for inheritance tax purposes; if debenture or loan stock is quoted ex-interest, the interest (less tax at the appropriate rate) must be included.

Unquoted stocks and shares

The basis upon which stocks or shares that are not quoted on a recognised stock exchange are valued depends upon the percentage of the company's share capital held by the taxpayer. A shareholding of 50% or less is valued according to the dividend yield; a holding of between 50% and 90% on an earnings yield basis; and a holding of 90% or over on an assets basis.

Life policies

If the occasion for the valuation of the life policy is the policyholder's death, the value is the sum paid out by the life assurance company, but if the transfer occurs upon any other occasion the value is the open market value at which the policy could be sold (not the surrender value which will usually be less).

Related property

Related property is property which would have an increased value if owned with other property that is:

◆ owned by the taxpayer's spouse or civil partner, or

◆ was owned within the last five years by a charity, housing authority, political party which qualifies for exempt transfers, or an institution specified in the amended Schedule 3 of the Inheritance Tax Act 1986 (roughly speaking, bodies to which exempt transfers can be made such as national, local and university museums and art galleries, the National Trust and other bodies established for the preservation of the national heritage), to which it was transferred by the taxpayer or his spouse or civil partner after 15 April 1976.

An example will assist: suppose a taxpayer owns a set of antique chairs and his wife owns a matching table. The set of chairs and the table will be worth more in total as a set than they would be worth when owned separately and even though the taxpayer may have bought his at an auction and wife inherited hers, they will be related property for inheritance tax purposes.

Related property is valued in special ways when calculating inheritance tax. There are what is known as the General Rule

Method and the Special Rule Method. The General Rule Method is used when the items of related property have different attributes, e.g. the chairs and the table, and the Special Rule Method is used when the items are identical, such as shares of the same class of shares in a company which is an investment company and accordingly not entitled to business relief.

To ascertain the inheritance tax valuation of an asset using the General Rule Method, apportion the combined value of the assets in proportion to their value as separate items or to put it another way, divide the asset's normal value by the total of its normal value and the normal value of the related property and multiply the result by their combined value.

To ascertain the inheritance tax valuation of an asset using the Special Rule Method, the apportionment is based upon the quantum and not the value of each asset. Therefore in the case of holdings of the same class of shares in a company it does not matter, for example, that one of the holdings is a majority shareholding and the other holding is a minority holding (shares in a majority holding being worth more than shares in a minority holding); all that matters is the number of shares in each holding. To ascertain the value of a holding, divide the number of shares held in the holding by the total number of shares in the holding and the related holding, and multiply the result by the value of the combined holding.

Land, shares, unit trusts and common investment funds sold within a short time of death

If the values of shares (other than those quoted on the Alternative Investment Market – AIM), unit trusts, common investment funds and land or buildings fall during the period of the administration of an estate, and in the course of administration of the estate they are transferred to a beneficiary or sold at a loss compared with their value at the date of death, it is possible to have the value revised to reflect the fall.

It should be borne in mind that if assets are revalued for inheritance tax purposes to reflect a fall in value between the date of death and the date they are disposed of by transfer to the beneficiary or sale, the reduced value becomes the base cost (i.e. the value at which the assets are deemed to have been acquired by the transferee or beneficiary) for capital gains tax purposes.

To obtain agreement by the Revenue to a revaluation in the case of stock exchange securities and unit trusts, the personal representatives must have sold them within 12 months of the date of the death. To recalculate the amount of tax properly payable, the loss is deducted from the declared value of the estate and is calculated by deducting the gross proceeds of sale from the value declared for probate purposes. No allowance is made for the expenses of sale and all the quoted investments in the estate must be revised, not merely those sold at a loss. If the personal representatives reinvest the proceeds of sale by buying further unit trusts or quoted investments within two months of the last sale during the 12-month period, the amount of repayable tax will be restricted.

Similar principles apply in the case of land or buildings, the differences being that the period for the sale is four years instead of 12 months; the period for reinvestment is four months after the last qualifying sale in the period of four years from death instead of two months during the period of 12 months from death and sales at a profit in the fourth year after death or which result in a profit or loss of less than 5% or £1,000.00, whichever is the lower, are ignored.

Grossing up gifts
Inheritance tax payable on immediately chargeable lifetime gifts is payable by the donor unless the donor and the donee agree otherwise. If the tax is to be paid by the donor the gift must be 'grossed up' for the purpose of calculating inheritance tax; that is to say the gift is considered to be the amount of the gift and the tax because that is the amount by which the donor's wealth is diminished. If additional tax becomes payable because the donor dies within seven years of the making of the gift, it is always payable by the donee.

The wording of a will can decide who pays any inheritance tax referable to a gift contained in the will. Unless the gift is one of jointly owned or foreign property, if the will does not state that any tax in respect of the value of the bequest is to be paid out of the bequest, i.e. that it is given 'subject to tax' as opposed to 'free of tax,' any tax in respect of it is borne by the residuary estate. If the residue of the estate is exempt from inheritance tax because it is left to an exempt beneficiary such as a registered charity or a spouse, any legacies given 'free of tax' are 'grossed up' and treated for inheritance tax purposes as a legacy of the stated amount and the tax. The Revenue will have its pound of flesh!

The rates of tax
Current inheritance tax rates, exemptions and allowances can be obtained from the Inland Revenue and Customs website www. hmrc.gov.uk.

4

Reserving a Benefit from Gifts and the Pre-owned Assets Income Tax Charge

THE MEANING OF RESERVATION OF A BENEFIT

If a taxpayer makes a gift but 'reserves a benefit' to himself from the gift, the asset given is still considered to form part of his estate as long as he benefits or is entitled to benefit from it. A person is considered to reserve a benefit from an asset if he continues to have the use of it or to benefit from it in any way after it has been given, without making monetary payment for the use or benefit at a full commercial rate.

Moreover, a gift is not considered to have been completely made until the donee takes possession of the subject matter of the gift. By way of example, if someone tells his friend that he gives the friend a picture or antique table and the picture or table is not taken away and remains in the donor's house, as long as the picture continues to hang on the donor's house wall or the table is not taken away, then the donor is considered to reserve a benefit from the gifts, both because the donor continues to have the use of them and because the donee has not taken possession of them to the virtual exclusion of the donor. If a person is considered to reserve a benefit because possession or enjoyment of the subject of the gift is not assumed by the donee at least seven years before the death of the donor, or if at any time within that period the property given is 'not enjoyed to the entire exclusion or virtually to the entire exclusion of the donor,' the subject matter of the gift given will form part of the donor's estate.

In effect the donor is considered to reserve a benefit if he keeps back any significant benefit from the property given away (unless he pays a commercial rent or hire charge for the benefit) and he will gain no tax benefit in respect of the gift because it will be counted as still owned by him and part of the value of his estate. If the benefit ceases at a date after the gift was first made, it ceases to be a gift with a reservation from the date the benefit is lost and, of course, a transaction in which a donor taxpayer paid a commercial rent or hiring charge for the benefit for a time and then stopped will become a gift with a reservation from the time the payments ceased.

The Revenue takes a strict view of what constitutes reservation of a benefit and has said that it considers there is a reservation of a benefit in any case where the benefit is 'significant' in relation to the value of the property given. By way of example the Revenue has stated that in the case of a gift of a house it does not consider that:

- visits to a house for domestic reasons, for example baby-sitting by the donor for the donee's children, or

- staying in the house in the absence of the donee, for not more than two weeks each year, or

- staying in the property with the donee for less than one month each year, or

♦ staying temporarily while the donor convalesces after medical treatment, or while the donor looks after a donee convalescing after medical treatment or while the donor's own home is being redecorated,

would cause the value of the gift to be included in the donor's estate, but staying in the house most weekends or if a property which had been given is used by both the donor and the donee as a holiday or second home on an occassional basis would.

A taxpayer cannot have his cake and eat it. To be a tax-effective gift what is given must go almost in its entirety and no real benefit can be retained, even by a behind-the-scenes arrangement.

It is wise to avoid making a reservation from a gift because not only is the subject of the gift considered to remain in the estate of the giver but it is also considered to be in the estate of the recipient for inheritance tax purposes.

THE PRE-OWNED ASSETS INCOME TAX CHARGE

Various complicated schemes (usually based upon the use of trusts) have been marketed to avoid the inheritance tax liability resulting from the gifts with a reservation of an interest rules. As with any artificial arrangements which are solely for the purpose of saving of tax, a taxpayer should think carefully before entering into them because they have a habit of rebounding upon him. In his budget of March 2004 the Chancellor of the Exchequer outlined proposals for a 'free standing income tax charge' based on 'pre-owned assets' to counteract such schemes and 'the benefit people get from having free or low cost enjoyment of assets they formerly owned or provided funds to purchase'. If a scheme succeeds in avoiding the liability for inheritance tax that results from the reservation of a benefit rules, liability to income tax is likely to be incurred under the pre-owned assets charge.

The nature of the charge

The pre-owned assets tax charge is similar to the income tax charge made upon employees for benefits in kind supplied by their employers and quantifies in cash the annual benefit enjoyed. A financial sum is attributed to the benefit and that sum is added to the taxpayer's income for calculating his income tax, but if the cash value of the benefit is less than £5,000 it is disregarded.

The proposals were enacted into law by Schedule 15 of the Finance Act 2004 and apply from 6 April 2005 and to all gifts made after 17 March 1986.

What incurs the charge

The charge applies to both tangible and intangible assets. It also applies to any funds or contributions to the funds used to acquire the assets from which the donor benefits and whether the funds or contributions are directly or indirectly provided. It applies therefore to assets which have been given, to assets which have been acquired by cash which has been given and to any assets which have been acquired by the use of money raised by using assets which have been given, e.g. by selling or mortgaging them.

In the case of those who are or are deemed to be domiciled in United Kingdom, the charge applies to their assets anywhere in the world and in the case of others only to their assets in the United Kingdom.

Calculating the charge

The amount of the income tax charge is a sum equivalent to the annual rental value of the asset in the case of land or buildings and in the case of other assets to a rate of interest on a notional loan of a sum equal to the market value of the asset, and in each case less any payment made under a legally binding agreement for the use of the asset. After the deduction of the amount paid for the benefit, the sum so ascertained is added to the taxpayer's taxable income and taxed at his top rate of tax. The first £5,000 per annum is ignored but once the £5,000 exemption is exceeded, the exemption is totally lost.

The market value is that which exists at the date the benefit starts and must be revised periodically. The current rate of interest is set out in the *Charge to income tax by Reference to Enjoyment of Property previously owned Regulations 2005* (Statutory Instrument Number 724).

Exceptions from the charge

The income tax charge does not apply if:

♦ the asset ceased to be owned before 18 March 1986

♦ the formerly owned asset is currently owned by the taxpayer's civil partner or spouse (their domiciles are irrelevant for this exception)

♦ the asset was transferred to a spouse, former spouse, civil partner or former civil partner by court order

♦ the entire asset was sold for its cash value in a transaction on arm's length terms whether or not the parties were connected persons

- the owner of the asset was formerly the owner of the asset only by virtue of a will or intestacy which has subsequently been varied by agreement between the parties, i.e. by a Deed of Family Arrangement, as explained in Chapter 8

- the asset is land or buildings which have been given and the donor and the person to whom it is given share the occupation of the land and either the donor pays all the running costs and capital expenses relating to the occupation of the property or an amount at least proportionate to his share of the ownership and use of the property so that he cannot be said to be retaining any benefit from the arrangement

- the gift does not take the asset out of the donor's taxable estate for inheritance tax purposes, e.g. a gift to a company in which the donor owns all the shares or the asset still counts as an asset of the donor for inheritance tax purposes under the gift with a reservation rules

- any benefit is no more than incidental, including cases where an out-and-out gift to a family member comes to benefit the giver as a result of a change in their circumstances, for example, a case where a parent gives a house to a child and several years later, because of ill health, needs to move into the house to live with the child so that the child can care for the parent

- the gift is an outright gift of money used to acquire land or another asset made seven years or more before the earliest date upon which the donor either occupied the land or had the use of the asset

- the original gift was for the maintenance of the donor's family or within the small gifts exemption (£250 per donee) or within the inheritance tax annual gifts allowance (£3,000 in total) as set out on pages 13 and 14

- the donor is not resident in the United Kingdom

- the asset which gives rise to the benefit is situated abroad and the donor does not have his domicile in the United Kingdom

- the asset is a non-UK asset which the taxpayer ceased to own before he became domiciled in the United Kingdom

- the aggregate benefits do not exceed £5,000 in one year.

Former owners are not regarded as enjoying a taxable benefit if they retain an interest which is consistent with their ongoing enjoyment of the property. For example, the charge will not arise if an elderly parent formerly owning the whole of their home passes a 50% interest to a child who lives with the parent. It could well apply if the parent gave a 90% interest to the child and might also apply if the child did not live with the parent.

JUMPING OUT OF THE PRE-OWNED ASSETS TAX PAN INTO THE INHERITANCE TAX FIRE

If the taxpayer so elects before 31 January after the end of the first tax year in which the pre-owned asset rules apply to him (the relevant filing date), he can choose to have the property concerned treated as part of his estate for inheritance tax purposes as a gift with reservation of an interest rather than have the benefit taxed as income. In those circumstances, the property would be eligible for the normal inheritance tax reliefs and exemptions available; for example, to quick succession relief, business and agricultural property reliefs and to relief for heritage assets. As to these reliefs, please see the next chapter. The election, which can be withdrawn before the relevant filing date while the chargeable person is alive, is made to the Capital Taxes Office on its specified form.

Whether it will be advantageous for a taxpayer to opt into inheritance tax by reason of the transaction being a gift with a reservation of a benefit instead of paying the pre-owned asset income tax charge will depend upon how long he has to live, the amount of the income tax charge and the rate at which his income is taxed. If the taxpayer does consider opting out of the pre-owned asset regime and to be taxed on the basis of the gift with a reservation, it might be worthwhile comparing the cost of the premiums for a life policy to cover the cost of the anticipated inheritance tax with the amount of the income tax which it is anticipated will be charged. If a policy is to be taken out, the insurance company should be requested to write the policy in trust for those who will bear the inheritance tax liability so that the policy monies will not themselves be taxed as forming part of the deceased's estate and will be available to pay the inheritance tax payable before a grant of representation is granted.

If a taxpayer gives an asset away and pays a full commercial rent or hiring fee to use it, although doing so will save inheritance tax, it will not usually be an otherwise tax-efficient transaction because as far as income tax is concerned, the taxpayer will be paying the rent or hiring fee out of taxed income and the recipient of the gift will have to pay income tax on the rent. Moreover, if the taxpayer's principal private residence is the subject of the transaction, the capital gains tax exemption for a principal private residence will be lost when the donee comes to dispose of the property, unless during the period of the donor's benefit the donee also uses it as his principal private residence.

Whenever a gift is made the capital gains tax and income tax implications as well as the inheritance tax implications of the transaction must always be considered. If the taxpayer is liable to the pre-owned asset charge he should declare the benefit in the 'any other income' section of his income tax return.

5

Inheritance Tax Reliefs

WHAT INHERITANCE TAX RELIEFS ARE

There are certain circumstances and certain types of property in respect of which relief is given against inheritance tax and it is either reduced or not charged at all. The principal reliefs are listed below.

Taper relief

In the case of gifts made between three and seven years before death, only a proportion of the tax is charged, the proportion depending upon how long the taxpayer survives the making of the gift. This reduction in the inheritance tax is known as taper relief.

♦ At the time of writing (2007), if the taxpayer survives the making of the gift by seven years or more, 100% relief is given and no inheritance tax is payable in respect of the gift.

♦ If the survival period is between six and seven years, tax is payable in respect of the gift at 20% of the death rate, i.e. at the rate of 8%.

♦ If the period is between five and six years, tax is payable in respect of the gift at 40% of the death rate, i.e. at the rate of 16%.

♦ If the period is between four and five years, tax is payable in respect of the gift at 60% of the death rate, i.e. at the rate of 24%.

- If the period is between three and four years, tax is payable in respect of the gift at 80% of the death rate i.e. at the rate of 32%.

Note it is the tax itself that is reduced and not the value transferred.

Business property relief

The nature of the relief
Business property relief operates to reduce, for inheritance tax purposes, the value transferred by a transfer of:

- 'relevant business property'
- in a qualifying business
- which has been owned throughout the two years immediately preceding the transfer

by 100% or 50% and it operates whether the property is situated here or overseas.

What is relevant business property?
Business property includes not only land and buildings, but also the other assets of a qualifying business, provided that they are 'relevant business' assets and not 'excepted assets' and they have been owned throughout the relevant period. The relief operates by reducing the value transferred and the amount of the reduction depends upon the type of relevant business property concerned.

Business property entitled to 100% relief
Relevant business assets which are entitled to 100% relief consist of:

- a business or a share of a business, such as a share in a partnership

- shares in a company which are not quoted on a recognised stock exchange (although shares which are traded on the Alternative Investment Market [AIM] do benefit from 100% relief)

- securities which are not quoted on a recognised stock exchange and which are owned by the transferor and either by themselves, or when combined with other unquoted shares or securities he owns, give him control of the majority of the voting rights in the company

- assets of a trust which the person presently entitled to use them under the terms of the trust (the life tenant) uses in the business.

Business property entitled to 50% relief
Relevant business property entitled to 50% relief consists of:

- securities or shares in a company which are quoted on a recognised stock exchange and which are owned by the transferor and either by themselves or when combined with other quoted shares or securities he owns, give him control of the majority of the voting rights in the company

- land, buildings, plant and machinery owned by the transferor and used immediately before the transfer, mainly or wholly by a qualifying business in which the transferor is either a controlling shareholder or a partner.

Excepted assets

'Excepted assets' are assets that have not been used wholly or mainly for the purpose of the business throughout the preceding two years or are not required for an identified future use in the business, e.g. investments of the business or excessive cash balances. Parts of buildings or land which are used exclusively for the business, are treated separately and may be considered for business relief and not as excepted assets.

If the 'relevant business property' is a business itself or a share in a business it should be noted that it is the business or share in the business itself and not the business's individual assets which must have been owned for two years.

Which businesses are qualifying businesses?

To qualify for the relief the business must be one that is carried on for profit and the relief does not apply to businesses wholly or mainly engaged in dealing in securities, shares, land or buildings or the making or holding of investments, although the business of a market maker or discount house in the United Kingdom qualifies for business relief. Neither does the relief apply to businesses or business property which are subject to a contract of sale at the relevant time, unless the sale is in return for shares in the acquiring company which will continue the business. Therefore the relief does not apply to a share in a partnership if it is a term of the partnership deed that the partnership share must be sold to the remaining partner or partners.

Calculation of the time condition in special circumstances

Death within seven years of the making of a lifetime transfer

If a transferor dies within seven years of making a transfer, inheritance tax may become payable, or if tax has already been paid at the rate applicable to lifetime dispositions, further tax may become payable. Business property relief applies if various additional conditions are fulfilled.

For business property relief to be available in these circumstances, the original asset must have been owned by the transferee throughout the period between the original transfer and the death of the transferor (or the death of the transferee if earlier) and must be relevant business property at the time of such death. The rate of relief is that in force at the date of the transferor's death.

Replacement assets
Assets which replace other assets that would qualify for the relief but for the two-year ownership condition qualify for the relief if both periods of ownership occur in the five years immediately preceding the disposition and taken together amount to two years or more.

In cases where tax or additional tax becomes payable in respect of replacement assets on a lifetime transfer because of the death of the transferor within seven years of the lifetime transfer, the following additional conditions must be complied with if relief is to be available:

- the sale and purchase must be at arm's length and take place in a period of not less than three years of each other

- the entire sale proceeds must have been used to purchase the replacement property.

Assets inherited from a spouse or civil partner

In the case of assets inherited from a spouse or registered civil partner, the period during which the spouse or civil partner owned the assets can be included to make up the period of two years.

Disposals on death

The two-year rule does not apply to otherwise qualifying relevant business property which was entitled to relief when it was acquired by the current transferor, his spouse or civil partner, if either the current disposal or the earlier disposal was or is made on death.

AGRICULTURAL PROPERTY RELIEF

The nature of the relief

In many ways agricultural property relief resembles business property relief. It operates to reduce for inheritance tax purposes the agricultural value transferred by a transfer of the asset by 100% or 50% and does not apply if the asset is under a binding contract for sale at the time of the disposition. The relief applies only to the agricultural value of the property transferred, i.e. it does not apply to the value which the property would have if it were used, or could ever be used, for any purpose other than agriculture. Consequently the value of an asset for the purpose of calculating agricultural property relief is sometimes less than its value as a business asset. If agricultural assets form part of a business, although double relief is not possible, it is sometimes possible to claim business relief on the excess of their business value over their value as agricultural assets.

The time conditions

Except for the situation set out in the next paragraph and when the transferor dies within seven years of the transfer discussed later on pages 49–50 the transferor must either have occupied the property for agricultural purposes for the two years immediately preceding the disposition or it must have been owned by the transferor throughout the period of seven years immediately preceding the disposition and occupied for agricultural purposes by the transferor or someone else throughout that period. If the property was inherited upon the death of a spouse or registered civil partner, the period of ownership and occupation by the spouse or civil partner can be included when computing the periods of occupation or ownership as the case may be, and occupation by a transferor-controlled company counts as occupation by the transferor.

If the property was entitled to agricultural relief when it was acquired by the transferor, by his civil partner or his spouse and was either acquired on a death or the present disposition occurs on a death, relief applies without the necessity for complying with the time conditions provided that the property is occupied for agricultural purposes by the person making the second disposition or was so occupied by the personal representatives of the person from whose estate it was acquired.

Replacement assets

Assets which replace other qualifying assets and which would qualify for the relief but for the condition relating to ownership and occupation for agricultural purposes by the transferor for two years, qualify for the relief if the period of ownership and occupation of both assets occur in the five years immediately preceding the disposition and taken together amount to two years or more.

Assets which replace other qualifying assets and which would qualify for the relief but for the condition relating to ownership by the transferor and occupation for agricultural purposes for seven years, qualify for the relief if the period of ownership and occupation of both assets occur in the ten years immediately preceding the disposition and taken together amount to seven years or more.

However, as with business property relief, in cases where tax or additional tax becomes payable in respect of replacement assets on a lifetime transfer because of the death of the transferor within seven years of the lifetime transfer, the following additional conditions must be complied with if agricultural property relief is to be available:

- the sale and purchase must take place in a period of not less than three years of each other

- the entire sale proceeds must have been used to purchase the replacement property

- the property must not be subject to a binding contract for sale

- the original asset must have been owned by the transferee throughout the period between the original transfer and the death of the transferor or the death of the transferee if earlier

- the original property must be agricultural property immediately before the death of the transferor or the earlier death of the transferee and occupied for agricultural purposes throughout the period between the transfer and the death.

The rate of relief is that in force at the date of the transferor's death.

What kinds of agricultural property qualify for the relief?
Agricultural property relief only applies to certain agricultural property situated in the United Kingdom, the Isle of Man or the Channel Islands. It does not apply to property situated elsewhere.

The agricultural property concerned is defined as follows.

♦ Agricultural land.

♦ Woodlands and buildings occupied with agricultural land which are used for the intensive rearing of livestock or fish if the occupation is ancillary to the use of the agricultural land. To be ancillary to the use of the agricultural land the woodland or buildings as the case may be, must be used as a subordinate part of the farm: there must be a common purpose for the occupation of the agricultural land and the buildings or woodland to which both contribute and the use of the buildings or woodland must be subsidiary to the overall agricultural activity carried on on the land.

♦ Farmhouses and other farm buildings which are of a size and character appropriate to the requirements of the farm concerned and farm cottages occupied by agricultural employees of the farm.

If the size of the 'farmhouse' is disproportionate to the size of the land being farmed with it and more like a country house, it will not be considered to be a farmhouse and not be entitled to agricultural property relief. The house must be ancillary to the farmland. The question to be decided is whether the holding is a farm or a house with land. Is it merely a place where the farmer of that farm lives or, in the words of one judge, 'a considerable residence'?

Similarly if the owner of the 'farmhouse' lives in it but lets the land to another who farms it, the 'farmhouse' will not be entitled to agricultural property relief because it will not be a farmhouse in the true sense of the word in that it is not occupied for the agricultural purpose of farming the land. The extent to which the person who occupies the 'farmhouse' must be involved in the actual day-to-day working of the land to retain the 'farmhouse's' entitlement to agricultural relief is an interesting but unresolved question. Is it sufficient that the occupier retains general control of the strategy and running of the farm and is entitled to its fluctuating profits while contracting out the day-to-day work on the farm to a manager, or must the occupier actually carry out the farming processes in person? Perhaps the best way of looking at the question is to ask how great a convenience or necessity it is for the occupier of the house to live there if he is to carry out the functions he carries out in connection with the farming of the land?

◆ growing crops transferred with the relevant land

◆ stud farms for horses and associated pasture

◆ land which is part of a habitat scheme

◆ controlling shareholdings which meet the time test in farming companies that also meet the two or seven year test in relation to the qualifying assets of the companies, but only to the extent that the agricultural value of the companies' qualifying assets is represented in the shareholding.

To calculate the proportion of the value of the shares in respect of which agricultural relief is available, divide the value of the company's eligible assets by the value of its total assets and multiply the resulting figure by the value of the shares. Agricultural property relief is not given in respect of shareholdings in such companies other than controlling shareholdings and is not given in respect of any value other than the agricultural value. Nor is it given in respect of assets that are not eligible assets.

It should be noted that agricultural relief does not apply to agricultural machinery or stock.

The rate of the relief
The agricultural value of the asset transferred is reduced by 100% agricultural property relief if:

♦ the transferor had owner occupation or the right to obtain vacant possession within 24 months, or

♦ the interest is an agricultural tenancy which commenced on or after 1 September 1995, or

♦ the case is the unusual one of land let on a tenancy commencing before 10 April 1981 in respect of which certain conditions apply and in respect of which transitional relief is given at 100%.

In all other cases the relief is given at 50%.

Mortgaged property

If a mortgage is secured upon agricultural and non-agricultural property, it is necessary to apportion the amount of the mortgage between the agricultural value of the agricultural property and the full commercial value of the non-agricultural property in proportion to the respective values and then deduct the respective apportioned amounts of the mortgage from the respective gross values to ascertain the net value of each part. Agricultural relief at the appropriate rate is then applied to the net value agricultural value of the agricultural part and the resultant figure is then added to the net value of the non-agricultural property to ascertain the total value upon which inheritance tax is to be charged.

Agricultural Property Relief when the transferor dies within seven years of the transfer

If a transferor dies within seven years of making a transfer, inheritance tax may become payable, or if tax has already been paid at the rate applicable to lifetime dispositions, further tax may become payable. Agricultural property relief applies if various additional conditions are fulfilled.

For agricultural property relief to be available in these circumstances:

♦ the property must not be subject to a binding contract for sale

♦ the asset must have been owned by the transferee throughout the period between the transfer and the death of the transferor or the death of the transferee if earlier

♦ the property must be agricultural property immediately before the death of the transferor or the earlier death of the transferee and occupied for agricultural purposes throughout the period between the transfer and the death.

The rate of relief is that in force at the date of the transferor's death.

In cases where tax or additional tax becomes payable in respect of **replacement assets** on a lifetime transfer because of the death of the transferor within seven years of the lifetime transfer, the following additional conditions must be complied with if relief is to be available:

◆ the sale and purchase must be at arm's length and take place in a period of not less than three years of each other

◆ the entire sale proceeds must have been used to purchase the replacement property.

Agricultural and/or Business Property Relief?

If assets qualify for both agricultural relief and business relief, only one relief is given and that relief is agricultural property relief. If farm assets do not qualify for agricultural property relief, for example a farmhouse on a French farm or livestock on any farm, they might still qualify for business property relief if the appropriate conditions are met.

Woodland relief

In some circumstances an individual can obtain temporary relief from inheritance tax on his death on the value of timber growing on land (other than agricultural land) within the United Kingdom, but not on the value of the land upon which the timber is growing. Throughout the five years prior to his death the deceased must have owned or had an interest in possession (such as a life interest) in the land upon which the timber is growing or he must have been given and not purchased it. This condition is to prevent deathbed purchases of woodland being used as a tax-avoidance measure. The relief is not available for lifetime disposals and must be claimed by an election made within two years of the death unless the Revenue is prepared to exercise its discretion and accept an election made at a later date.

Woodland relief does not apply to shares in companies which own woodlands and is seldom used because the conditions for business relief or agricultural relief can usually be complied with.

On a later disposal of the timber (other than to a spouse or registered civil partner) inheritance tax is payable on its net value at the time of disposal but at the rate applicable on the deceased's death, unless the rate has been reduced, when the appropriate rate is that applicable at the date of the disposal. The value of the timber is likely to be higher then than at the time of the deceased's death. In calculating the net value, the expenses of replanting the woodland within three years and the expenses incurred in disposal can be deducted if they are not claimable for income tax.

Quick Succession Relief
Quick succession relief is given when someone dies and his estate has been increased by a taxable disposition in his favour within the previous five years. The idea is to reduce the tax payable on the second transfer of assets within the five years. It is not essential for the property given by the first disposition to have

been retained by the person concerned until the time of the second disposition.

The relief operates by reducing the tax payable on the second occasion by a sum equal to a percentage of the tax paid on the first occasion in respect of the increase in value of the second estate by the asset concerned. The increase is calculated on the basis of the net increase after deduction of tax and allowing for reliefs such as business relief but without any deduction for the expenses of administering the estate. It is a tax credit and it is the tax payable that is reduced, not the value of the asset. The percentage depends upon how long has elapsed between the two dispositions:

- if less than one year has elapsed the percentage is 100%
- if between one and two years have elapsed the percentage is 80%
- if between two and three years have elapsed the percentage is 60%
- if between three and four years have elapsed the percentage is 40% and
- if between four and five years have elapsed the percentage is 20%.

Relief for Heritage assets

Limited conditional relief is given in respect of land, buildings and objects which appear to the Treasury to be of outstanding importance from the point of view of the national heritage. The relief is dependent upon specified obligations designed to preserve the asset and afford public access to it in this country being undertaken by the donor.

Death and military service

If someone dies, or his death is hastened, as a result of a pre-existing disease which is aggravated during active military service or as a result of a wound incurred, a disease contracted or an accident which occurred on active military service, no inheritance tax is payable. By concession the relief is also allowed for the estates of members of the Royal Ulster Constabulary who die as the result of injuries caused by terrorist activity in Northern Ireland.

Relief for land and other assets sold within a short time of death

It is sometimes possible to adjust for inheritance tax purposes the value attributed to any stock exchange securities (other than those quoted on the AIM market), shares in common investment funds, unit trusts, and land or buildings which are sold in the course of administration of the estate at a loss compared with their value as declared in the probate papers, to reflect the sale price rather than the value at the date of death.

To obtain agreement by the Revenue to a revaluation in the case of stock exchange securities, shares in common investment funds and unit trusts, the personal representatives must have sold them within 12 months of the date of the death. To recalculate the amount of tax properly payable, the loss is deducted from the declared value of the estate and is calculated by deducting the gross proceeds of sale from the value declared for probate purposes. No allowance is made for the expenses of sale and all the investments of this description in the estate must be taken into account, not merely those sold at a loss. If the personal representatives reinvest the proceeds of sale by buying further unit trusts, common investment funds or quoted investments within two months of the last sale during the 12-month period, the amount of repayable tax will be restricted.

Similar principles apply in the case of land and buildings, the differences being that the period for the sale is four years instead of 12 months; the period for reinvestment is four months after the last qualifying sale in the period of three years from death instead of two months during the period of 12 months from death; and sales at a profit in the fourth year after death or which result in a profit or loss of less than 5% or £1,000 are ignored.

Deeds of Family Arrangement and distributions made from discretionary trusts made within two years of death

It is possible for the beneficiaries of a will, or those who inherit a share of an estate upon an intestacy, to vary the terms of the will or the inheritance on intestacy by agreement after the death. This is done by a voluntary agreement contained in a document known as a Deed of Family Arrangement or by a deed of disclaimer. Similarly, the personal representatives of a beneficiary who survives his benefactor and then dies can vary the inheritance if they have the consent of those who benefit under his will or upon his intestacy. These matters are dealt with in some detail on pages 111 onwards. If special provision were not made to the contrary, any such variation would constitute a taxable disposition and transfer of value. However, the Inheritance Tax Act comes to the rescue and provides that if the variation is made within two years of the death and certain other specified conditions are complied with, the transfer shall not be considered to be a transfer of value and the variation is to be viewed from an inheritance tax point of view as if it had been made by the deceased. Distributions made within two years of a testator's death from discretionary trusts created by his will are also considered to have been made by the deceased's will.

Double taxation relief

If an asset which is situated overseas is subject to a tax similar to inheritance tax in the foreign country and also to inheritance tax in the United Kingdom, relief will be given as a credit against the United Kingdom tax payable in respect of the overseas asset. The relief given is the lower of the foreign tax which has been paid in respect of the asset and the United Kingdom tax which would otherwise be payable in respect of the asset, the United Kingdom tax being calculated at the average percentage rate payable in respect of the estate.

6

Trusts and Inheritance Tax

WHAT IS A TRUST?

A trust is an arrangement under which someone, who is called a trustee, holds or manages assets (the trust fund), of which he is considered to be the legal owner, under a legal obligation to use them for the benefit of a person, purpose or organisation (the beneficiary) or people, purposes or organisations (the beneficiaries), of whom the trustee may be one. The person who sets up the trust is called the settlor and the trust may be created by an express statement of the settlor (an express trust) or by implication from his conduct or presumed intention (an implied or resulting trust) or imposed by the law to achieve fairness in a particular situation (a constructive trust). This book is concerned mainly with express trusts. Although express trusts of assets can be created orally, they are usually created by a document such as a deed or will and the document which creates them is called the trust deed. The trust deed sets out the rules by which the trust is to be managed and defines the trust fund and the powers and the duties of the trustees. Each trust may have up to four trustees and they must be aged 18 or over and mentally capable. The trust deed also states who the beneficiaries are to be or defines them as being the members of a particular class, e.g. 'my grandchildren who are living at the date of my death'.

A trust has its own independent existence and is a separate legal entity, separate from the settlor, the trustees and the beneficiary.

THE ESSENTIALS OF A VALID TRUST

To be valid a trust must comply with what are known as the 'three certainties':

◆ certainty of words
◆ certainty of subject matter
◆ certainty of objects.

Certainty of words means that the words or conduct which are used to create the trust must show that it is intended to impose upon the trustees a legal obligation to use the trust fund for the beneficiaries; the words must be imperative and not merely an expression of wishes or hope.

Certainty of subject matter means that the property that is to be the subject of the trust and the extent of the benefit which each beneficiary shall have in it must be clearly defined or ascertainable. A trust of 'some of my paintings' is therefore void.

Certainty of objects means that the identity of the possible beneficiaries must be clear at the latest when the time comes to distribute the trust funds. A disposition for the benefit of 'my friends' will be ineffective.

INTEREST IN POSSESSION TRUSTS AND THEIR USES

The nature of an interest in possession trust

Limited interest in possession trusts (which for the sake of brevity are, in the following pages, referred to simply as interest in possession trusts) are trusts in which someone (technically known as the life tenant or tenant for life), has a **present or immediate** legal entitlement to benefit from the trust fund for his life or any other limited time (the interest in possession), after which the benefit will pass to another person.

The interest or right to benefit that will exist after the life tenant's interest ceases is known as the remainder or reversionary interest and the person to whom it will pass is known as the remainderman. There can be more than one tenant for life and more than one remainderman in a given trust at any one time.

Uses for interest in possession trusts

Interest in possession trusts are particularly useful in the case of second or subsequent marriages if a taxpayer wishes his assets to benefit his spouse after his death but to ensure that they are inherited by his children and no one else after her death. Thus a taxpayer might leave his house to trustees upon trust to provide a home for his widow (the tenant for life) during the remainder of her life and to be inherited by his children (the remaindermen) after her death. In this way he is able to provide for his widow but at the same time to extend the period during which he can control the destiny of his asset.

Interest in possession trusts are also useful to provide for the maintenance of individual children in a family until they are capable of providing for themselves. They are expensive from an income tax point of view if the income exceeds £100 per annum and the trust funds have been provided by a parent, as opposed to, say, by a grandparent, because in the former event (for income tax purposes) the income will be considered to be that of the settlor parent and the child will not be able to set his tax free and reduced rate income tax allowances against the income.

RELEVANT PROPERTY OR DISCRETIONARY TRUSTS, THEIR ADVANTAGES AND USES

The nature of a relevant property trust

A relevant property trust is a trust in respect of which no individual beneficiary has a **present or immediate** right to a defined part of the trust assets or of the income of the trust: the trustees have a **discretion** to divide them as the trustees think fit between any one or more beneficiaries (or class or classes of beneficiaries) specified in the trust deed. For this reason relevant property trusts are sometimes referred to as **discretionary** trusts. Until the trustees have made a decision and exercised their discretion, all the individual potential beneficiaries have is a hope or expectation of benefiting from the trust even though, in accordance with the general principles of trust law, if the potential beneficiaries all have full legal capacity they can collectively put an end to the trust.

A provision should be included in the trust deed of a discretionary trust to the effect that if, at the date the trust is to terminate, the trustees have not been given and used a power to allocate the trust fund to beneficiaries, a specified beneficiary or beneficiaries shall inherit the undistributed trust fund. If this is not done in the case of a trust created by the settlor during his lifetime, at the end of the trust period the trust fund will revert to the settlor and he will be considered for inheritance tax purposes to have reserved a benefit from the gift of the trust assets to the trust when he created it.

Some trust deeds give the trustees wide powers to decide who shall benefit from the trust funds at any given time but identify specific people or causes to benefit from the funds unless and until the trustees exercise those powers. The trusts created by such deeds are sometimes referred to as hybrid trusts and in truth may be interest in possession trusts or discretionary trusts at different times during their existence and taxed accordingly. The test at any moment of time is 'has a particular person or group of people or cause, an immediate **right** to income from the trust fund for a limited period?' If the answer is yes, an interest in possession trust is in existence; if no, a discretionary trust.

Letters of wishes

It is the usual practice for the settlor of assets on a discretionary trust to leave a letter of wishes stating the principles the settlor wishes the trustees to use when deciding how to exercise the discretion they are given concerning the allocation of the trust fund and the income it produces. If the settlor leaves a letter of wishes great care must be taken in the drafting of the letter to ensure that the trustees' discretion remains legally unfettered and that they are free to ignore the settlor's wishes, otherwise the trust will be classed as an interest in possession trust and not as a discretionary trust.

Advantages and uses of discretionary trusts

The principal advantage of a discretionary trust is that no inheritance tax is charged upon the death of a potential beneficiary because no beneficiary has a right to any defined interest in the trust assets or the income they produce until the trustees have exercised their discretion in his favour.

A further major benefit of discretionary trusts is flexibility. Within the wide boundaries set out in the trust deed a discretionary trust permits the trustees to use the trust fund in the way they consider to be most appropriate having regard to the circumstances which exist at the times they make their decisions. The circumstances at these times might be very different from those that existed at the time the settlor set up the trust and considered his objectives.

Discretionary trusts are frequently used to provide for people whose financial needs are likely to vary at different times in the future or to protect the trust fund from creditors if one of the potential beneficiaries is a spendthrift or engaged in hazardous business ventures and likely to become bankrupt.

THE TWO-YEAR DISCRETIONARY WILL TRUST

A particularly useful provision is contained in section 144 of the Inheritance Tax Act 1984. This section in effect provides that if a discretionary trust is created by a will, transfers made not less than three months and not more than two years after the death of a testator out of the trust can be treated as being dispositions made by the will and made directly by the testator. It should be noted that if trustees of a two-year discretionary will trust use their discretion to allocate capital and choose that the allocation shall be considered as having been made by the testator in his will, the recipient will be considered to acquire the allocated assets for the purposes of capital gains tax at the base value which exists at the date of the allocation and not that which existed at the date of the testator's death. Any gain or loss in the value of the relevant trust asset between the date of the death and the date of the allocation will be considered to be that of the trust for capital gains tax purposes.

TAXATION OF TRUSTS IN GENERAL

For UK taxation purposes, a trust is a separate legal entity and the trustees of a trust are considered as a continuing body distinct from the individuals who compose it. A change of trustee does not have any tax implications. Generally speaking the trust has its own taxation rates, limits and exemptions. However, if the settlor or the settlor's spouse or registered civil partner might benefit from the trust, income and the capital gains of the trust are considered to be those of the settlor although taxed in the hands of the trustees at the rate applicable to trusts, unless the income is distributed income which is taxed at the dividend trust rate.

Taxation of a trust must be considered in respect of inheritance tax, capital gains tax and income tax and at three stages: when assets are transferred into the trust, during the continuance of the trust, and when assets are transferred out of the trust including when it finally terminates. Different types of trust are taxed differently and it is therefore important to know to which class of trusts a particular trust belongs and which trust taxation system applies to it.

The law has traditionally applied one of two different systems or regimes of taxation to trusts. The first system is that which applied to 'relevant property' trusts and the other system is that which applied to 'limited interest in possession trusts'.

THE TAXATION OF TRUSTS BEFORE 22 MARCH 2006

An outline of the taxation of relevant property trusts

In summary the relevant property trust tax regime consists of:

◆ an immediate charge to tax at the lifetime inheritance tax rate (at the time of writing 20%) upon any funds that exceed the inheritance tax threshold which are transferred into the trust during the settlor's life – this is known as the '**entry charge**'

◆ a '**periodic charge**', levied on every tenth anniversary of the creation of the trust, of a maximum of 6% of the sum by which the value of the trust fund exceeds the inheritance tax threshold

◆ an '**exit charge**', which is levied when assets are taken out of the trust between the ten-year anniversaries and which is proportionate to the periodic charge, the proportion depending upon the time that has elapsed since the last ten-year anniversary.

Tax on the creation of relevant property trusts – the entry charge
The transfer of assets into a new or existing relevant property trust is a transfer of value for inheritance tax purposes.

Unless the transfer is one of the statutory exempt transfers or the assets are excluded property, a lifetime transfer of assets into a discretionary trust which causes the settlor's nil-rate band to be exceeded will be immediately chargeable with tax at one-half of the rate applicable to transfers on death. Transfers into relevant property trusts are not PETs.

If the discretionary trust is created by the taxpayer's will on his death, the assets which become part of the trust are treated as part of the taxpayer's estate and the normal inheritance tax rules apply.

Capital gains tax is charged in accordance with the normal capital gains tax rules when an asset is put into a discretionary trust by a settlor during his lifetime, but because there is no capital gains tax on death, no capital gains tax is charged when a discretionary trust is created by the testator's will.

The ten-year periodic charge to inheritance tax
Every ten years during the life of a discretionary trust there is a periodic charge to inheritance tax on the value of the 'relevant property' immediately before the tenth anniversary of the commencement of the trust that falls after 31 March 1983. Subject to very minor and infrequent exceptions, 'relevant property' is the settled property, i.e. the trust funds of the discretionary trust (other than property held only for charitable purposes and excluded property) in which there is no interest in possession subsisting.

The rate at which the periodic charge to tax is charged is three-tenths of the rate at which tax would be charged on a lifetime transfer of:

◆ the assets of the trust fund

◆ any other settlement made by the same settlor which began on the same date

made by a person who had a cumulative total of transfers equal to the total of those made by the settlor in the **seven** years prior to the commencement of the trust and any capital which has been transferred out of the trust in the previous **ten** years.

EXAMPLE

The calculations are complex and may perhaps best be understood by considering an example:

On 1 January 1996 a taxpayer created a discretionary trust with a trust fund of £200,000, having made transfers of £95,000 in the previous seven years. On 1 January 2000 the trustees used a discretion which had been given to them to make a capital payment of £140,000 from the trust to one of the potential beneficiaries. On 1 January 2006 the value of the trust fund was £80,000.

The ten-year periodic charge is calculated as follows.

The value of the trust fund on the date of the hypothetical ten-year anniversary transfer	£80,000

Cumulative total of the settlor's transfers and the distribution which had been made from the trust £95,000 + £140,000 = £235,000

Rate of tax at lifetime rate on a transfer of £80,000 with a hypothetical previous cumulative total of £235,000 equals:

Total transfers £80,000 + £235,000 =	£315,000
Deduct nil-rate band	£300,000
	£15,000

Tax on £15,000 at 20% = £3,000
Rate of tax equals 3,000 divided by 80,000 multiplied by 100% = 3.75%.
The ten- year periodic charge rate is therefore three-tenths of 3.75% = 1.125% and the tax charged is 1.125% of £80,000 = £900. ∎

The maximum ten-year charge at current rates on assets which have been in the trust fund for a full ten years is 6% of the value of the asset i.e. three tenths of the current lifetime inheritance tax rate of 20%.

TAX TIP

If possible it is better to make lifetime gifts after and not before transferring assets to a discretionary trust because if made after, the gifts would count as PETs and the transferor might survive long enough to enable them to become exempt transfers. If the gifts are made before the transfer to a discretionary trust, the gifts will be counted in the settlor's cumulative total of transfers made in the seven years prior to the commencement of the trust when calculating the ten-year charge.

The periodic charge is intended to produce an amount of tax equivalent to that which would normally be produced in respect of the trust fund in other circumstances over a generation.

The discretionary trust inheritance tax exit charge
The exit charge to inheritance tax applies when the trust fund or a part of the trust fund ceases to be subject to discretion, for example when a capital payment is made from the trust fund to a beneficiary. A payment from the trust which is paid to someone and is income of that person for the purpose of UK income tax, or which leaves a discretionary trust because it is used to pay expenses relating to relevant property, is exempt from an exit charge.

The inheritance tax exit charge differs depending upon whether the trust fund or part of the fund (as the case may be) ceases to be subject to discretion before the first ten-year anniversary or after the first ten-year anniversary of the creation of the trust.

Exit charges before the first ten-year periodic charge
If assets are transferred out of the trust before the first ten-year anniversary, the charge is made upon the value of the assets transferred out and ceasing to be subject to the trustees'

discretion. If the tax is to be paid by the trustees as opposed to being paid by the recipient, that value must be grossed up at the effective rate of the tax. The effective rate of tax is calculated on the basis of a hypothetical transfer of the value of the funds in the trust and in any other settlement made by the same settlor which began on the same date, immediately after the trust was created and by a settlor and with a cumulative total of transfers equal to those of the creator of the trust in the seven years before it was created. The tax is charged at three-tenths of the effective rate and according to the number of completed quarters which have elapsed between the date the assets entered the trust and the date they left, proportionate to ten years, i.e. at one-fortieth of three-tenths of the effective rate for each complete quarter.

EXAMPLE

Consider the following example:

On 25 March 2005 the settlor, who had made a cumulative total of £175,000 transfers in the previous seven years, transferred £200,000 into a discretionary trust and paid the inheritance tax out of his own pocket. On 30 September 2005 the trustees made a payment of £50,000 to a potential beneficiary, it being agreed that the beneficiary would pay the tax. The calculation of the tax payable is as follows:

The settlor's cumulative total of transfers	£175,000
Add the value of the trust funds at its creation	£200,000
	£375,000
Deduct the then nil-rate band	£300,000
	£75,000
Tax on £75,000 at 20% (the lifetime rate) =	£15,000

The effective rate of tax is (15,000 divided by 200,000 multiplied by 100%), and equals 7.5%.

The tax charged to the beneficiary is 30% of one-fortieth of the effective rate of 7.5% multiplied by the number of quarters (2) on the value of the payment out (£50,000), and equals £56.25. ■

Exit charges after the first ten-year periodic charge
If the trust fund or part of the fund is transferred out of the trust by the trustees exercising their discretion or ceases to be subject to discretion after the first ten-year periodic charge, tax is charged at the rate of one-fortieth of the previous periodic charge rate for each complete quarter that has elapsed between the previous anniversary charge and the date of the present exit charge.

The tax is charged upon the difference between the value of the fund before the disposition and its value after the disposition. If the tax is to be paid by the trustees out of the trust assets, as opposed to being paid by the recipient, the value must be grossed up at the effective rate of tax.

Because no individual potential beneficiary of a discretionary trust is considered to own a defined share of the trust fund or the income it produces, no inheritance tax charge arises on the death of a potential beneficiary of the trust.

The taxation of interest in possession trusts created before 22 March 2006
The creation of an interest in possession trust before 22 March 2006 by a settlor during his life was treated as a PET, but after that date a lifetime transfer of assets into a trust incurs an immediate charge to tax at the rate applicable to lifetime transfers if it causes the settlor's cumulative total of chargeable transfers to exceed the nil rate band, unless it is a transfer to a trust for the

disabled. If an interest in possession trust was created by the taxpayer's will or by an intestacy on his death, the assets which became part of the trust were treated for inheritance tax purposes as part of the taxpayer's estate and the normal inheritance tax rules applied. When an asset was put into an interest in possession trust by a settlor during his lifetime, capital gains tax was charged in accordance with the normal capital gains tax rules, but because there was no capital gains tax on death, no capital gains tax was charged when an interest in possession trust was created by the testator's will or upon his intestacy.

For inheritance tax purposes the tenant for life of an interest in possession trust was treated as the owner of the trust fund during his lifetime. Consequently on the death of the life tenant, unless the trust fund consisted of excluded property, the value of the trust fund was added to the value of his estate and inheritance tax charged on the total sum, subject to the usual exceptions and with the benefit of the usual reliefs. There was an exception to this rule in the case of reverter to the settlor trusts. In the case of reverter to the settlor trusts the value of the trust fund was not added to the tenant for life's estate if the trust fund reverted to the settlor, to the settlor's UK-domiciled spouse or if the settlor had died, to his UK-domiciled widow within two years of the settlor's death.

If more than one person were entitled to the income of the trust at a given time they were treated as owning the trust fund in the same proportions as their respective entitlement to the income of the trust. Thus if three people were entitled to share the income of the trust equally, on the death of one of them his estate was taxed as if it included one-third of the value of the trust fund.

If the life tenant disposed of his interest during his lifetime he made a transfer of value and inheritance tax was charged on the same proportion of the value of the fund as his income bore to the total income of the fund. The usual inheritance tax exceptions and reliefs applied and the disposition was a PET unless the disposition was to a discretionary trust, in which case it was immediately chargeable at the rate applicable to lifetime gifts (one-half of the death rate) to the extent that the taxpayer's nil-rate band had been fully used. The disposal might give rise to a capital gains tax charge being made upon the tenant for life depending upon what other disposals he had made during the relevant tax year.

A transfer of a reversionary interest did not cause inheritance tax to be charged because reversionary interests are usually excluded property. Nor was there any capital gains tax on a transfer of a reversionary interest unless the remainderman had purchased it. It was therefore a good idea, from an inheritance tax and capital gains tax planning point of view, for a remainderman who was comfortably off and satisfied that he would not require his reversionary interest to pass it on during his lifetime.

If an interest in possession trust itself disposed of trust assets, the capital gains tax regime applied and the trust was taxed on any gains made by the trust that exceeded its annual tax-free limit. This also applied if a beneficiary of a trust (other than a bare trust) became entitled to assets from the trust and it applied whether the trust was an interest in possession trust or a discretionary trust. However, there was an exception in that capital gains were treated as the settlor's in the case of trusts for the benefit of the settlor's children who were under age, unmarried and did not have a civil partner. The tax-free limit for trusts other than bare trusts (which do not have a tax-free allowance) in any given tax year is one-half of that which applies to an individual. If the trust disposed of a residential property occupied by the tenant for life as his sole or principal residence, capital gains tax private residence relief applied.

The income of an interest in possession trust was considered to be the income of the tenant for life and taxed accordingly unless the income from the asset exceeded £100.00 and had been settled by a parent upon a child who was under age, unmarried and did not have a civil partner, in which case all income from the asset was taxed as the income of the parent.

THE TAXATION OF TRUSTS AFTER 22 MARCH 2006
The rules relating to inheritance tax and trusts were radically changed in 2006, making trusts in many ways much less attractive as tax-planning vehicles.

The taxation of interest in possession trusts which existed on 22 March 2006
The rules for the taxation of interest in possession trusts which existed on 22 March 2006 continue to apply to such trusts after 22 March 2006 until the life tenancy which existed at that date comes to an end. Therefore if the life tenancy comes to an end because of the death of the life tenant, the value of the trust fund is added to the value of his free estate and inheritance tax charged accordingly. If the life tenancy comes to an end while he is still living, e.g. because he surrenders it to the beneficiary next entitled under the terms of the trust deed, the termination of the life

interest will count as a PET by the life tenant if the trust funds pass to an individual or to a trust for the disabled, but if they continue to be held on any other type of trust the termination counts as an immediately chargeable transfer by the life tenant into a new relevant property trust.

Additionally, if after 22 March 2006 a life tenancy which existed at 22 March 2006 terminates before 22 March 2008 and is immediately followed by another life tenancy; or a life tenancy which existed at 22 March 2006 ends after 22 March 2008 and is immediately followed by a life tenancy in favour of the deceased life tenant's spouse or civil partner, then the rules for the taxation of interest in possession trusts which existed before 22 March 2006 continue to apply to such trusts until the termination of the second life tenancy.

In all other circumstances, if the trust continues after the termination of the life interest that existed on 22 March 2006, the termination of the life tenancy is considered to create a new trust to be taxed as a relevant property trust unless it is a charitable trust or a trust for the disabled. For example, if the terms of the trust were that the trust fund was to be held for A during his life and then for A's son B during B's life and then for C, A's death after 22 March 2008 is considered as creating a new post-21 March 2006 trust.

The taxation of trusts created on or after 22 March 2006
Unless legislation provides otherwise, all trusts created on or after 22 March 2006 are subject to the relevant property regime which before that date applied only to discretionary trusts.

Trusts created on or after 22 March 2006 by a settlor in his lifetime
The only trusts created on or after 22 March 2006 by a settlor in his lifetime which are exempt from the relevant property taxation regime are trusts which are totally for charitable purposes as defined by the law, and trusts which qualify as trusts for the disabled. To qualify as disabled under section 89 of the Inheritance Tax Act 1984 a beneficiary must either be:

◆ unable to administer his or her property or manage his or her affairs because of mental disorder within the meaning of the Mental Health Act, or

◆ in receipt of either attendance allowance or in receipt of disability living allowance by virtue of entitlement to the care component at the highest or middle rate

and not less than half of the settled property which is distributed during his life must be applied for his benefit.

A trust for the disabled includes a trust made by someone in his own favour in the expectation of future disability.

Trusts for the disabled are usually written as discretionary trusts. The discretion given to the trustees enables them to adjust payments within limits according to the beneficiary's needs and the financial limits for any local authority or social security benefits the beneficiary might be receiving. While the trust fund is held on discretionary trusts for the disabled person, it is treated for inheritance tax purposes as if he owned it and any distribution of capital to him is not considered to be a transfer of value and is not subject to an inheritance tax charge. Neither does the ten-year periodic charge to inheritance tax apply. When property ceases to be subject to the trustees' discretion or when the disabled person dies there is a charge to inheritance tax as if the trust were an interest in possession trust.

Placing money in a trust for the disabled for a person unable to administer his property or manage his affairs because of mental disorder avoids the cumbersome and expensive involvement of the Office of the Public Guardian in his affairs in relation to the money.

Taxation of trusts which come into existence on death on or after 22 March 2006
Trusts which come into existence on death, i.e. upon an intestacy or under the settlor's will, on or after 22 March 2006 are subject to the relevant property trust taxation system unless they fall into one of the following categories.

♦ Trusts for the disabled.

♦ Trusts for bereaved minors, i.e. trusts for the benefit of an under-age child who has lost at least one of his parents and who will become fully entitled to the trust funds at an age which is not greater than 18. While the bereaved minor is under the age of 18 any capital used for the benefit of a beneficiary must be used for the benefit of the bereaved minor and no income of the trust can be used for the benefit of any other person. The trusts must be created by the settlor's will or on his intestacy, by a parent, step-parent or other person who has parental responsibility for the child or created under the Criminal Injuries Compensation Scheme. After any inheritance tax due on the parent's death has been paid there is no further inheritance tax payable.

◆ 18–25 trusts. These are trusts which do not qualify as trusts for bereaved minors solely by reason of the fact that the beneficiary does not become entitled to the trust funds at the age of 18 or under. However, the beneficiary must become entitled to the trust funds at an age not greater than 25. While the beneficiary is under the age of 18 there is no liability for periodic ten-year anniversary charges and no exit charge upon payments made to a beneficiary who is under the age of 18 or on attaining that age. Payments to a beneficiary who is over the age of 18, or on the beneficiary's death between the ages of 18 and 25, incur an exit charge which is calculated in the usual way from the date at which the beneficiary became 18.

◆ Immediate post-death interest trusts, i.e. trusts created on death for a life tenant whose interest begins immediately on the death. These trusts are taxed as pre-March 2006 interest in possession trusts and on the death of the life tenant the trust funds are aggregated with the life tenant's free estate for inheritance tax purposes. If the life tenant is the settlor's surviving spouse or civil partner, the surviving spouse exemption applies. If the life tenant terminates his interest, e.g. by surrendering it, the termination will be an immediately chargeable lifetime transfer if the trust continues, unless the continuing trust is a trust for charitable purposes or for the disabled or a bereaved minor's trust, in which cases the termination of the life interest will operate as a PET by the life tenant. If the termination of the life interest puts an end to the trust, the termination is a PET by the life tenant.

BARE TRUSTS, CHARITABLE TRUSTS AND LIFE POLICY TRUSTS

Before leaving the discussion of different types of trust there are three kinds of trusts which deserve special mention: bare trusts, trusts for charitable purposes and life policy trusts.

Bare trusts

What are bare trusts?
A bare trust is a trust which exists when an asset is in the name of one or more people but is not to benefit them but is for the benefit of others – nothing more and nothing less. Its main use is to hold property when it would not be practical for legal or other reasons for the beneficiary to have the property in his own name; for example, if the beneficiary is under age or mentally incapable of managing it himself or where it is desired to hide the identity of the beneficiary.

The taxation of bare trusts
When property is placed in the trust for the benefit of someone other than the settlor there is a transfer of value from the settlor/transferor's estate for inheritance tax purposes and whether and if so how the transfer will be taxable depends upon the rules previously discussed.

In the case of a bare trust, while the asset is in the trust, any income it produces and any income paid out is ultimately taxed as that of the beneficiary, unless:

◆ the asset was provided for the trust by a parent and the trust is for the benefit of an unmarried child who has not entered into a civil partnership and is under the age of 18 and

◆ the income produced by the asset is in excess of £100.00 per annum, in which case the whole of the income from the asset is taxed as that of the parent.

While the income is accumulating within the trust it is taxed as the trust's income at the rate applicable to trusts.

For capital gains tax purposes a bare trust is not considered to exist independently of the settlor or the beneficiary. Any capital gains made by the trust are considered to be those of the beneficiary, who is considered for capital gains tax purposes as the owner of the trust fund, unless a parent provided the trust asset and the beneficiary is an unmarried under-age child who has not registered a civil partnership, in which case the gain is treated as a gain by the parent. Because the beneficiary of a bare trust is considered to be the owner of the property for the purposes of capital gains tax, the capital gains tax exemption allowance to be applied is the full one for an individual and not the half-rate allowance given to other trusts.

When the asset leaves the trust, because the asset is considered to be that of the beneficiary, there is no transfer of value for inheritance tax or capital gains tax purposes if it is transferred out to the beneficiary. If it is transferred to some other person, e.g. on the beneficiary's death or upon his instructions during his lifetime, there will be a transfer of value to be taxed in accordance with the usual inheritance tax rules and unless the transfer is a transfer on death, a disposal for capital gains tax purposes. Holdover relief for capital gains tax is not available when transferring assets into or out of a bare trust.

Trusts for charitable purposes

What are charitable purposes?
Charitable purposes as defined by the law are purposes for:

- ◆ the relief of poverty, or
- ◆ the advancement of education or religion, or
- ◆ other purposes beneficial to the community.

There must be a substantial public element even in the first two classes to make a purpose or cause charitable in the eyes of the law; a trust to preserve the settlor's children from poverty or to educate them is not a charitable trust. The definition is due to be considerably widened when the remainder of the Charities Act 2006 comes into force (anticipated early 2008) but there will still be a requirement of public benefit which will not be presumed.

Taxation of trusts for charitable purposes
Gifts for the purposes of charity as defined by the law are exempt from inheritance tax if made in favour of a charity or charitable trust established within the United Kingdom, whether given during the taxpayer's lifetime or by his will. Inheritance tax is not payable while trust assets are held exclusively for charitable purposes, but if the trust deed provides that the trust assets are to be held by the trustees for the charitable purpose for only a limited period, an inheritance tax exit charge (albeit at a reduced rate depending upon how long the trust fund has been held for charitable purposes) will be payable when the assets cease to be held for charitable purposes. There is no inheritance tax exit charge levied when a discretionary trust makes a distribution to a charity.

Similarly, a donor does not incur a liability to capital gains tax in respect of any increase in the value of an asset over the price he paid for it if he gives the asset directly to a charitable trust, but if he sells the asset and makes a gain and then donates the proceeds of the sale to the trust, the gain will be taxable in his hands. A donor making a gift of an asset directly to a charitable trust cannot claim any capital gains tax loss; to do so he must first sell the asset and then donate the proceeds to the trust.

Charitable trusts do not incur any capital gains tax upon any gains they make in the course of their charitable activities or liability to income tax in relation to their non-business activities. Charities can reclaim any tax deducted at source from income of their non-business activities, but they can no longer claim the tax credit attached to dividend income received from their investments. The taxation of any trading income of a charity is complex and if a charity wishes to carry on a business-for-profit activity it will usually carry on the activity through a wholly owned subsidiary company which will covenant to donate its profits to the charity.

Life policy trusts

Life interest in possession trusts of life policies in existence at 22 March 2006 continue to be treated under the rules for taxation of interest in possession trusts which were in force before that date and the same applies to life interests which come into force on the death of a preceding life tenant of such trusts as long as there is no break in the chain. Premiums paid by an individual to such trusts continue to be PETs. Life policy trusts created after 22 March 2006 are taxed under the relevant property trust regime but because of their value, most premiums paid to new life policy trusts on their creation or during their existence may well be exempt under the annual gifts allowance, the £250 individual gifts exemption or as regular gifts made out of income which do not reduce the donor's standard of living.

TRUSTS: CAPITAL GAINS TAX AND INHERITANCE TAX

When considering effecting a transaction in the context of inheritance tax planning it is always necessary to bear in mind the cost of the transaction including the possibility that it will give rise to a capital gains tax liability at that time or in the future which will render the transaction inefficient from a taxation point of view.

The subject of capital gains tax deserves a book on its own and has indeed had several books devoted solely to it. No passing reference can do the subject justice or be thoroughly accurate and although detailed treatment of the subject is not possible in the context of this book, when considering inheritance tax and especially tax planning, it cannot be ignored. I make no pretence that what follows or what has been written above is a comprehensive summary of capital gains tax, but I trust that it will act as a signpost to any reader who has no previous knowledge of the subject.

How capital gains tax works

Capital gains tax is charged when an asset that is not exempt from the tax is disposed of, and is charged upon any increase in the value of the asset (the gain) between the date of its acquisition and its disposal. From the gain it is permissible to deduct the cost of acquiring the asset, increasing its value, defending one's title to and disposing of the asset, and taper relief is usually claimable to reduce a gain dependent upon the length of time that the asset has been owned. It is proposed that taper relief will be abolished at the end of the current tax year 2007/8. There is a minimum annual total of gains (currently £9,200 per individual or per trust for the disabled or £4,600 for other trusts) below which the tax is not charged.

Assets which are exempt from the tax include:

- UK government stock
- Savings Certificates
- Premium Bonds
- assets held in PEPs
- assets held in ISAs
- cash held in sterling
- foreign currency held for personal use
- chattels valued at £6,000 or less
- private motor cars
- the taxpayer's principal private residence with land in total not exceeding one half a hectare.

The payment of capital transfer tax due can be postponed by claiming holdover relief in certain circumstances.

Capital gains tax on a death

No capital gains tax is payable by a deceased person's personal representatives at the time of the death on the assets of the estate and for the purposes of capital gains tax the personal representatives are deemed to acquire the assets at their probate valuation. The transfer of assets from the deceased to his personal representatives which occurs on the death of a taxpayer is not considered to be a disposal of the assets for the purposes of capital gains tax and neither is the transfer of the assets from the personal representatives to the beneficiaries who again are deemed to acquire them at the probate valuation. If the personal representatives dispose of assets to anyone other than the legatees during the course of the administration of the estate (for example, if they sell assets to raise funds to pay debts), there is a disposal and a potential liability to capital gains tax, but the estate can claim the individual's annual exemption allowance for the tax year in which the death occurs and the two subsequent tax years.

Capital gains tax and trusts

Trusts (other than bare trusts and settlor interested trusts) are treated as separate entities for the purpose of capital gains tax and transfers into and out of trusts are treated as disposals. In the case of a bare trust the assets of the trust are considered to be those of the beneficiary. In the case of a settlor interested trust any capital gains tax liability of the trust is considered to be that of the settlor. A UK settlor interested trust for capital gains tax purposes is one from which the settlor or his spouse, civil partner or unmarried, under-age children who are not or have not been in a civil partnership can benefit.

The rate of capital gains tax charged in the case of a bare trust is that of the beneficiary unless the beneficiary is the settlor's child who is under age and has not married or entered into a civil partnership, in which case the gain is taxed as though it were the settlor's. Because the beneficiary of a bare trust is considered to be the owner of the property for the purposes of capital gains tax, the capital gains tax exemption allowance to be applied is the full one for an individual and not the half-rate allowance usually given to other trusts.

In the case of an interest in possession trust or relevant property trust, capital gains are assessed as those of the settlor if the settlor or his spouse or civil partner retains an interest in the trust or the settlor's under-age child who has not married or entered into a civil partnership is a beneficiary; otherwise they are taxed at the rate applicable to trusts. The rate of capital gains tax applicable to trusts is currently 40%.

Hold-over relief can be claimed when transferring assets into interest in possession trusts and relevant property trusts, provided that they are not bare trusts or settlor interested trusts. Hold-over relief means that the payment of any capital gains tax on the transfer is postponed until the assets transferred are disposed of by the trust and at that time taper relief is calculated by reference to the original cost to the settlor and the time that has elapsed since the date the settlor acquired them although it is proposed to abolish taper relief for capital gains tax on 5 April 2008.

$$\left(7 \right)$$

Who is Responsible for Payment of Inheritance Tax, Who Bears the Tax and When is it Payable?

PRIMARY AND SECONDARY RESPONSIBILITY FOR PAYMENT OF THE TAX

There are primary and secondary liabilities for the payment of inheritance tax. If the Revenue cannot, or chooses not to, extract the tax from the person primarily responsible for payment when it is overdue, the Revenue can obtain payment from the person who has the secondary liability for payment of the tax.

In cases where the tax is primarily the responsibility of the transferor there are secondary liabilities for payment upon the person to whom the asset is transferred (whether it is put in his name for his own benefit or the benefit of another) and upon anyone who benefits from it.

However, there are limits to a person's liability to pay the tax which in essence come down to the principle that a person is only responsible for the tax to the extent that the relevant assets come into his hands or would have come into his hands but for his neglect or default. There is an exception to this rule, the exception being that on death all the inheritance tax due in respect of an asset can be recovered from anyone entitled to an interest in the asset as a result of the death, for example from a person entitled to only a part of the income produced by the asset.

If a person who has the secondary liability for the payment of the tax pays it or a person with no responsibility for the tax pays it, he can recover the tax from the person further up the ladder.

TAX ON IMMEDIATELY CHARGEABLE TRANSFERS

Inheritance tax payable on an immediately chargeable transfer is borne by the donor unless the donor and the donee agree otherwise and, if borne by the donor, the gift must be 'grossed up', that is to say, the gift is considered to be the sum given and the amount of the tax payable because that is the amount by which the donor's estate is diminished.

ADDITIONAL TAX ON IMMEDIATELY CHARGEABLE GIFTS AND PETs WHEN THE DONOR DIES WITHIN SEVEN YEARS

Primary responsibility for payment of inheritance tax is usually that of the transferor but any tax which becomes payable on an immediately chargeable gift as the result of the death of the donor within seven years of the making of the gift is primarily the responsibility of the person to whom the gift is given or the person who receives a benefit from it, irrespective of who paid the tax which was originally payable. Similarly any additional inheritance tax payable on a PET by reason of death of the donor within seven years of the making of the gift is primarily the responsibility of the person to whom the gift is given or who receives a benefit from it. In these two cases, if the tax has not been paid to the Revenue within 12 months of the death, the Revenue can also recover it from the deceased's personal representatives out of the estate.

TRUST FUNDS AND TRANSFERS OF VALUE

If trustees make a transfer of value, any inheritance tax payable is

usually the responsibility of the trustees to be paid out of the trust
funds, but if a transfer of value is the result of the death of a
disabled person entitled to the income of a trust for the disabled
for the duration of his life, the tax payable on the death is borne
by the deceased's personal representatives and the trustees in the
proportion to the relative values of the deceased's own estate and
the trust funds. To work out the proportions, calculate an estate
rate by dividing the total inheritance tax payable by the value of
the total chargeable estate (the taxpayer's own assets and the trust
funds in which he had an interest) and multiply the resulting
figure by 100. Then multiply the value of the taxpayer's own
assets by the estate rate to ascertain the tax payable by his estate
and multiply the value of the trust funds by the estate rate to
ascertain the amount of the tax to be borne by the trust.

TAX ON A RESIDUARY ESTATE BEQUEATHED TO BOTH EXEMPT BENEFICIARIES AND TAXABLE BENEFICIARIES

If a will leaves the residuary estate to exempt beneficiaries (such as
a charity or a surviving spouse or civil partner) and to taxable
beneficiaries, any inheritance tax which is payable on the estate
must be paid out of the shares of the taxable beneficiaries after
the estate has been divided but before it is distributed. By way of
example, consider a will which gives a residuary estate of £500,000
before tax equally between the deceased's son and his widow and
in respect of which £90,000 tax is payable. Notwithstanding any
provision in the will to the contrary as to how they shall bear the
tax, the residuary estate must first be divided: £250,000 for the son
and £250,000 for the widow and then the full £90,000 tax must be
deducted from the son's £250,000 before the estate is distributed
so he will receive £160,000 and the widow £250,000. This is in

spite of the fact that the wording of the will provided that they should inherit equally.

TAX ON OTHER BEQUESTS MADE BY WILL

With the exception of the last mentioned rule the wording of a will can determine who bears any inheritance tax on bequests made by the will. Unless the will states otherwise, tax is borne by those who inherit the residuary estate except in the case of joint or foreign property, in which cases the tax is payable by the beneficiary of the jointly owned or foreign property.

SUMMARY

♦ **On a PET** (including a transfer of value into a trust for disabled beneficiaries) no tax is payable unless the donor dies within seven years, in which case it is payable by the donee and taper relief will be available if the donor survived the gift by three years or more.

♦ **On a lifetime immediately chargeable transfer** (such as a transfer of value into a trust other than a trust for disabled beneficiaries or a transfer to a company) if the transfer causes the transferor's nil-rate band to be exceeded:

a) The donor and the donee can agree who will bear the immediately chargeable tax but if it is borne by the donor the transfer will be treated as a gift of the sum given and of the relevant tax and the sum must be grossed up to ascertain the tax payable. The tax is payable at the lifetime rate which is one-half of the rate chargeable on death.

b) Any additional tax payable as a result of the donor dying within seven years of making the gift is the responsibility of and borne by the donee irrespective of who paid the immediately chargeable lifetime rate tax.

♦ **If trustees of a settlement make a transfer of value**, any
inheritance tax payable is the responsibility of the trustees to be
paid out of the settled funds, unless the transfer of value is the
result of the death of a person entitled to a present interest in
a trust for the disabled, in which case the tax payable on the
death is borne by the deceased's personal representatives and
the trustees in the proportion to the relative values of the
deceased's own estate and the trust funds. The tax is payable at
the estate rate.

♦ **If a will leaves the residuary estate between exempt beneficiaries
(such as charities, spouses or civil partners) and taxable
beneficiaries**, any inheritance tax which is payable on the estate
must be paid out of the shares of the taxable beneficiaries after
the estate has been divided but before it is distributed.

♦ **If a will does not state to the contrary, with the exceptions of
jointly owned assets, foreign property and residuary estates
bequeathed between exempt and taxable beneficiaries**, inheritance
tax is borne by the residuary estate.

WHEN IS INHERITANCE TAX DUE?

In the case of an immediately chargeable lifetime gift made
between 6 April and 30 September inclusive, the inheritance tax is
due on the 30 April in the following year and tax on immediately
chargeable gifts made between 1 October and 5 April becomes
payable six months after the end of the month in which the gift
was made.

If additional tax becomes payable in respect of an immediately
chargeable gift or inheritance tax becomes payable as a result of
the donor of a PET dying within seven years of the gift, the tax is

payable six months after the end of the month in which the donor dies.

All other inheritance tax payable as the result of death is payable on the earlier of the delivery of the account of the deceased's estate to the Revenue by the personal representative, or six months from the end of the month in which the death took place, whichever is earlier.

CAN INHERITANCE TAX BE PAID BY INSTALMENTS?

In respect of the following assets the tax can be paid by ten equal annual instalments if the transfer occurs on death, the first instalment becoming payable six months after the end of the month in which death occurred.

- land and buildings

- timber

- the net value of a business or an interest in a business as an entirety as contrasted with individual assets of the business

- controlling shareholdings in a company whether or not it is a quoted company

- holdings of unquoted shares whose minimum value is at least £20,000 and which represent at least 10% of the company's issued share capital or, if they are ordinary shares, 10% of the company's issued ordinary share capital

- holdings of unquoted shares in respect of which the tax cannot be paid in a single payment without undue hardship

- holdings of unquoted shares, if the tax on them and other assets for which payment by instalments is permissible exceeds 20% of the tax payable by one person in the same capacity.

If the tax is payable by the donee in respect of a PET of the above types of assets, the option to pay by instalments can also be claimed, but only if the assets are still owned by the donee at the date of the donor's death or the donee's earlier death and if they are unquoted securities they must also have remained unquoted throughout the entire period between the original transfer and the death.

When the asset is sold, or in the case of a trust asset it ceases to be held on trust, the instalment option ends and any unpaid tax becomes immediately payable.

INTEREST ON INHERITANCE TAX

Interest at a daily rate is charged on unpaid inheritance tax from the date it becomes due. In the cases of buildings and land which do not qualify for agricultural relief and shares in an investment or property company, interest is charged on the full amount of tax outstanding but in the cases of the other assets which have the benefit of the instalment option interest is only charged if the instalment is overdue. The present rate of interest is 5% per annum.

CALCULATING INHERITANCE TAX – A BRIEF SUMMARY

To calculate the inheritance tax payable on a non-exempt lifetime gift, deduct the balance of the tax threshold which remains unused by previous non-exempt gifts from the net value of the gift and apply the full tax rate to obtain the figure for the tax. Then apply taper relief to the resulting figure. Tax is only payable on lifetime gifts if the total of the chargeable gifts themselves exceeds the tax threshold, in which case apply taper relief to the tax, not to the value of the gift.

To calculate the inheritance tax payable on a death estate, add the total of the net death estate to the total of the chargeable lifetime gifts and deduct any unused balance of the tax threshold. Apply the full tax rate to the resultant figure and then deduct the full tax payable on the lifetime gifts (calculated as above before the application of taper relief).

8

Taking Steps During Your Life to Reduce Inheritance Tax

INHERITANCE TAX PLANNING IN CONTEXT

At the time of writing, when an estate incurs a liability to inheritance tax, the tax takes a substantial bite out of the taxable estate (20% in the case of lifetime transfers of value and 40% in the case of transfers which take place on death). This situation is not likely to improve and could get worse. In spite of this it is important to take a long-term view and keep in mind the bigger picture. Although reducing the tax liability is important for the sake of those who will be left behind, it is essential to bear in mind the effect of possible future inflation rates and not impoverish oneself. Do not go overboard on the subject or let the tail wag the dog!

The basic principle of taxation is that if you have it you shall pay your fair share. The principle is vividly illustrated by the pre-owned assets charge and the disclosure of tax-avoidance scheme rules introduced by the Finance Act 2004 to clamp down upon the evermore ingenious and artificial schemes produced by a growing army of tax advisers to avoid or reduce the inheritance tax take. As always the question is the interpretation of the word 'fair', with the judiciary on the one hand insisting that tax avoidance (the arranging of one's financial affairs within the law and for legitimate reasons so as to incur as little tax as possible) is to be upheld, and increasingly frustrated and frequently outwitted governments considering it 'unfair' and seemingly attempting to obliterate the concept and phrase 'tax avoidance' from the English psyche and language.

In spite of the conflict there is much that both parties agree can properly and safely be done between the battle lines that have been drawn up which will reduce inheritance tax liability. However, if you have read the preceding chapters, you will realise that inheritance tax is an extremely complicated subject and the path of tax avoidance is strewn with traps for the unwary and for the uninitiated. It is therefore only sensible (and one might say essential) to obtain a second opinion from a tax professional on any plan or step you envisage to check that it:

- has been approved by HM Revenue and Customs
- will reduce your inheritance tax
- is right for you

before taking action – but take some action you probably should and before it is too late. To check whether you need to take action, or are likely to need to take action, value your taxable estate in accordance using the principles and information set out on pages 23–31, make allowance for any reliefs referred to in Chapter 5, deduct the current nil-rate band and, if the result is a positive figure, read on.

SAVING INHERITANCE TAX BY MAKING GIFTS DURING YOUR LIFE

If the basic principle of taxation is that if you have it you pay, the basic principles of tax planning are to try to ensure that you do not have it at the relevant time, that what you do have consists as far as possible of assets that are favoured by tax exemptions or reliefs and that you have made provision for the payment of payable tax out of assets which are outside your estate.

Overcoming reluctance to give and early giving

Unfortunately it is necessary to retain a reasonable amount during one's lifetime and for any number of reasons, many people have a strong reluctance to giving. If you are one of them it will help if you remember that once your estate crosses the inheritance tax exemption threshold, your beneficiaries will be paying tax at a very high rate indeed on the excess and that any non-taxable gift you make, either in your lifetime or by your will, will only cost your estate £60 of every £100 given because the other £40 would have been payable to the Revenue as inheritance tax. It is important to make the best use possible of the inheritance tax gift exemptions. From a tax point of view, provided you do not impoverish yourself, it is an excellent idea to give away as much as you can in your lifetime and the sooner you give it, the more tax you will save. Non-taxable gifts of income-producing assets reduce both the donor's inheritance and income tax liabilities and if made at the appropriate time and judiciously chosen can also reduce future capital gains tax liability. Moreover, immediately taxable gifts made in the taxpayer's lifetime suffer inheritance tax at only one-half of the tax rate suffered by taxable gifts occurring on death, and gifts made during the taxpayer's lifetime which were not then immediately chargeable might escape tax altogether as PETs, or if they become taxable on his death might be taxable at a lower rate by reason of taper relief. The giver of a lifetime gift might also have the pleasure of seeing the recipient enjoy the gift and perhaps even make good use of it, something that it is debatable that he will be able to do after his death!

Using non-taxable dispositions, inheritance tax-exempt gifts and excluded property

The first thing to do when considering inheritance tax planning is to review the lists of non-taxable dispositions, inheritance tax-exempt gifts and excluded property set out on pages 7–10 and 12–15 and to see if the moment is ripe for using any of them.

Most reversionary interests are excluded property and therefore not included in the taxpayer's estate when calculating his inheritance tax liability. A taxpayer who is moderately well off and who is to inherit assets from a trust fund on the death of another person might wish to consider whether he is likely to need them or whether it might be better to transfer his reversionary interest in the fund while it is still reversionary (and therefore before it becomes taxable) to those he would wish to benefit in the future. Such a transfer (being a transfer of excluded property) does not give rise to any inheritance tax liability even if the transferor dies within seven years of making it.

When considering a gift always weigh up and balance the inheritance tax saving against the cost of any legal fees and consider the capital gains tax and income tax implications. Lifetime transfers by way of gift are exempt from stamp duty. Also remember that you cannot have your cake and eat it. To be a tax-effective gift it must go pretty well completely and you cannot retain any significant benefit from it either directly or indirectly, even by a behind-the-scenes arrangement.

Remember that both parties to a marriage or to a registered civil partnership have their own set of gift exemptions and that asset transfers to a spouse or registered civil partner are exempt from capital gains tax and stamp duty. Sharing assets with, or giving assets to, a spouse or registered civil partner who owns less than the inheritance tax threshold might enable the spouse or partner to make tax-free gifts to others from the assets which she might otherwise be unable to make and in this way use her otherwise unusable exemptions and at the same assist the person who makes the gift to his spouse or partner to reduce his own potential tax liabilities.

Making non-exempt gifts in excess of the inheritance tax threshold

When making a non-exempt gift in excess of the nil-rate band the hope is always to survive for more than seven years from the date of the gift so that the gift will be exempt, unless it is a gift to a trust which is subject to the relevant property taxation regime, in which case it will be subject to an entry charge at one-half of the rate which would be charged if the gift were made on death. If the donor does not survive for the requisite period some comfort can be taken from the facts that although the applicable rate of tax will be the rate at the date of death, the gift will be valued for the purposes of inheritance tax and capital gains tax at the value it had when it was made and taper relief will be available on the gift if the donor survived for at least three years. Moreover, the relevant tax exemption threshold is the one which exists at the date of death and that is usually higher than the one which existed when the gift was made.

A decreasing term insurance policy on the life of the donor to cover a period of seven years can be taken out as a precaution against the possibility of inheritance tax becoming payable on PETs. The insurance company should be asked to write the policy upon trust for the person who has the potential liability for the tax. This person is not necessarily the person who received the gift because gifts are set against and eat up the nil-rate band in chronological order. If the premiums on the policy are paid by the donor it is likely that payment of the premiums will be exempt from inheritance tax as being regular payment made out of the donor's income without decreasing his standard of living or that they can form part of the small gifts or annual gifts exemptions. If the donor does not take out insurance against the potential liability for tax, the donee or other person with the potential liability can take out cover because he will have an insurable interest in the life of the donor. Most inheritance tax is payable before the grant of representation to the estate can be obtained by the deceased's personal representatives and it is necessary for the personal representatives to obtain the grant to realise most assets, for example non-trust life or endowment policies taken out by the deceased. If the policy is written upon trust it will not be part of the deceased's estate and the policy monies will be available fairly quickly upon production of a death certificate without the necessity to produce a grant of representation to obtain them. They can then be temporarily loaned to the personal representatives of the deceased to pay probate fees and inheritance tax payable before the assets of the estate can be realised.

Although insurance costs can be high in the case of an elderly donor, decreasing term insurance is much cheaper than full life cover and if the donee does not have funds to pay any payable inheritance tax he might have to sell the asset given to raise the money needed to meet the tax bill.

Lifetime giving by spouses and civil partners who are terminally ill

If one spouse or partner becomes terminally ill, try to make use of the exempt lifetime gifts to the maximum as each tax year passes. Also use the fact that lifetime gifts between spouses or registered civil partners are exempt from both inheritance and capital gains taxes to ensure that any estate of the spouse or partner who is likely to die first which is not to be left to the survivor will exceed the exempt threshold by as little as possible; the survivor can then use his or her own lifetime gift exemptions to make gifts from the estate he or she inherits to the intended beneficiaries which would have been taxable if made on the first death.

Timing gifts into discretionary trusts and other gifts during lifetime

If possible it is better to make lifetime gifts to individuals after and not before transferring assets to a discretionary trust because if the gifts are made before the transfer of assets into the discretionary trust, the gifts will be counted in the settlor's cumulative total of transfers made in the seven years prior to the commencement of the trust when calculating the ten-year charge.

Choosing which assets to give and the beneficiaries

When deciding which assets to give, consider giving the asset which has the greatest growth potential because the asset given will be valued as at the date the gift is made and the gift of assets with the greatest growth between the date of the gift and the date of death will bring about the greatest reduction in the value of the estate for inheritance tax purposes. If it is possible to make such gifts to younger rather than older individuals, so much the better because in the normal course of things they will have longer to live before inheritance tax is payable on the recipients' death. If assets already have a large capital gain it might be worth retaining them and giving alternative assets (bearing in mind that there is no capital gains tax liability on death), unless they can be given away under the annual capital gains tax exemption limit.

Some think that whenever possible one should tend to retain assets which receive some inheritance tax relief, such as gifts of shares in unquoted companies which have been held for two years or more, business property, agricultural property and commercial woodlands, especially if they are producing a good income. Others consider that the reliefs accorded to these assets are over-generous and that they are the assets to give, bearing in mind that future legislation could revoke or modify them at any time. If they are given and there is a choice of beneficiaries, is it also preferable to give them to recipients who are likely to continue them and themselves benefit from the reliefs.

When choosing beneficiaries bear in mind the effect on any social security benefits they are receiving.

USING THE FAMILY HOME

Downsizing, equity release schemes, roll-up mortgages and home reversionary schemes

A taxpayer who wishes to make gifts while he is still alive in an effort to reduce the amount of inheritance tax payable on his death and who has insufficient liquid assets because his wealth is tied up in a family home, might wish to consider 'downsizing', or raising money upon the security of the home by means of an equity release scheme such as a roll-up mortgage (sometimes called a lifetime mortgage) or a home reversionary scheme.

To downsize is to sell the property and to move into a cheaper property. A roll-up mortgage is a mortgage in respect of which the borrower is not required to make repayments until the property is sold or the owner dies. In a home reversionary scheme the owner sells part or the entirety of the home and in either case on the understanding that he will be allowed to remain in it until he sells the fraction he had previously retained (if he has only sold a share in the property) or until he either goes into long-term care or dies. If he is married or has a partner, the property should be jointly owned and any roll-up mortgage or other equity release scheme should be entered into jointly so that the survivor will have the benefit of remaining in the property after the first death.

In any mortgage-based scheme a careful check should be made as to what interest rate is being charged and whether the interest rate is fixed or variable. The interest rates are usually higher in the case of roll-up mortgages than those charged on other types of mortgage. Check also whether the interest is calculated with daily, monthly, quarterly or yearly rests because over a period of years it can make a considerable difference to the amount of interest paid or the amount outstanding at the end of a roll-up mortgage. The effect of compounding interest can be alarming. In any scheme that involves an annuity, check whether the annuity is fixed or variable.

Anyone who proposes to enter into any of these schemes should also check:

◆ that he will be able to sell and move into another suitable property without terminating the scheme if, as a result of a change in circumstances, the existing property becomes unsuitable

- whether he will incur any, and if so what, penalty charge, if he wishes to terminate the scheme early for any reason

- that there is a guarantee that he (or his estate when he dies) will not be required to make up any deficiency if the value of the property becomes lower than the outstanding debt

- what effect any income he receives from the scheme or from investing any capital he obtains from it will have on his income tax position or means-tested benefits.

He should also remember that entering into an equity release scheme will possibly prevent a third party, such as a child or other carer, living with him. If it did not do so it would almost certainly necessitate the child or carer leaving and perhaps becoming homeless when the scheme terminated upon the homeowner's death or when it became necessary for the homeowner to enter into care.

Throughout the entire period of the scheme or of a roll-up mortgage, the homeowner will remain responsible for paying Council Tax and maintaining and insuring the property.

A homeowner who gives away cash which he received from an equity release scheme could possibly affect the chance of having his care home fees paid for him in the future and incur the pre-owned assets income tax charge on benefits he receives, at the time or in the future, from assets acquired by the donee by the use of the money.

Using the schemes provides liquidity and releases money which can then be used to make gifts or spend and thus reduce the

inheritance tax bill. At the same time, in the case of a
reversionary interest scheme, the value attributable to the property
in the homeowner's estate is less and therefore the tax bill is
further reduced; in the case of a roll-up mortgage a new
deductible liability is created and the bill reduced. If a roll-up
mortgage is used the householder retains ownership of his home
and benefits from the entirety of any subsequent gain in value.

It is essential to obtain independent legal and financial advice
before entering into any such arrangements and to note that legal
and surveyor's fees will be charged, although some, but not all,
companies will reimburse the fees if the scheme is completed.

Financial risks and dangers of other possible solutions based upon the family home

With the high prices of homes today a common problem for many
people is that the home forms a substantial proportion of the
taxpayer's wealth. There is insufficient cash or investments which
can be given away to make full use of the tax-exempt lifetime gifts
and the nil-rate band without impoverishing the taxpayer and/or
his spouse/partner and there is a great temptation to try to reduce
the value of the taxable estate that the taxpayer would leave on his
death by making lifetime gifts of the entirety or a share of the
family home but to continue to live there.

The financial services industry has dreamt up ingenious and
complex schemes to permit the taxpayer to continue to occupy his
home as long as he wishes but at the same time reduce or
eliminate its value for inheritance tax purposes on his death. Such
schemes are fraught with potential problems and if they are to be
entered into they should be entered into in the full knowledge that

they may well not succeed and if they do not do so it is the taxpayer's estate and not the financial service provider that will bear the loss. One has only to remember the introduction of the pre-owned assets charge which was brought in to counter artificial transactions solely entered into for the purpose of reducing tax and took effect retrospectively to upset transactions that had been effected, sometimes 19 years earlier, to realise that if such schemes do succeed they can be overturned by any government.

When considering any idea of disposing of the family home or a share in the home and residing there after the disposition (even if the taxpayer is to leave the home and return much later and whether the disposal be by way of gift or by sale), careful attention must be paid to the gift with a reservation and the pre-owned assets rules discussed in Chapter 4 and it is **essential** to take advice from a tax lawyer or tax accountant before acting. Traps for the unwary permeate this subject.

The government has stated that the pre-owned asset charge will not be considered to apply if the enjoyment of the benefit is only incidental, including cases where an out-and-out gift of the taxpayer's home to a family member comes to benefit the giver as a result in a change in the parties' circumstances. For example, if an elderly parent who gave the family home to a child and moved to separate accommodation is later compelled to return to the property which had been given by the need to be cared for by the child as the result of subsequent ill health or infirmity.

Former owners are not regarded as enjoying a taxable benefit if they retain an interest which is consistent with their ongoing enjoyment of the property. For example, the charge will not arise if an elderly parent who is the sole owner of his home passes a 50% interest to a child who continues to live with the parent and continues to pay a 50% share of the outgoings: a tax liability might well arise if the share were, say, 80% or the child did not live with the parent or the running costs were not shared proportionately. The proportions should probably be proportionate to the parties' use of the property as opposed to their shares of the ownership but this has not as yet been authoritatively decided.

Other possible solutions

Giving and leasing back
A possible partial solution to the problem for a taxpayer who wishes to dispose of his home but continue to live in it might be to make an outright gift of the property, followed by a leaseback of the property to the taxpayer at a full market rent or full market premium for seven years, but this idea has still to be tested in the courts. Even if it works, whether it is worthwhile must be judged by weighing the potential inheritance tax saving against the legal and rental costs of the operation and the loss of the capital gains tax exemption for the taxpayer's principal private residence. It should also be noted that the rent paid (out of the donor's taxed income) would be taxable in the hands of the donee.

Mortgaging and giving the mortgage monies
A taxpayer with a large amount of equity in his house who wishes to raise cash from the house for his own use or to give away with the object of reducing inheritance tax might wish to consider a mortgage, a remortgage or a further charge upon the security of

the property. To do so (unless the mortgage is a roll-up mortgage) he will need to be able to show how he proposes to repay the mortgage or further charge by supplying evidence of sufficient income sources which are likely to continue or producing an acceptable guarantor (perhaps an intended donee or a family member).

After making the gifts (if they are not covered by the gift exemptions or his unused nil-rate band) the taxpayer will hope to live for seven years from the date of the gifts so that they benefit from being PETs and he will perhaps take out term assurance to cover the risk of dying earlier. Such a course will reduce the tax on the estate if the taxpayer survives for three years or more (taper relief) and dies before repaying the mortgage, but it should be noted that unless a roll-up mortgage is used, the mortgage repayments, including interest, will be an additional living expense to the taxpayer who should take care not to impoverish himself. A roll-up mortgage will produce the greatest reduction in the taxpayer's estate.

Such a scheme might be open to attack by the Revenue under the rule against associated operations as defined in section 268(1) of the Inheritance Tax Act 1984, which is discussed later in this chapter in connection with the purchase of an annuity and life policies.

Selling subject to a right to occupy

In the unusual case of children who have sufficient funds which have not been provided either directly or indirectly by the parent, it is possible for the children to purchase the family home from the parent at the full market price and for the parent to continue to live there by reserving a right to do so from the sale. This transaction relies upon section 10(1) of Schedule 15 of the Finance Act 2004 which reads:

> 10 (1)...the disposal of any property is an 'excluded transaction' in relation to any person...if–
> ...it was a disposal of his whole interest in the property, except for any right expressly reserved by him over the property, either–
>   (i) by a transaction made at arm's length with a person not connected with him, or
>   (ii) by a transaction such as might be expected to be made at arm's length by persons not connected with each other.

Note that this exclusion only applies to a disposal of the seller's whole interest in the property and the scheme will not succeed if only a part of his interest is sold. Moreover, the transaction must be 'such as might be expected to be made at arm's length by persons not connected with each other' so that the full market price must be paid. The purchase money must be from the purchaser's own resources and not by money provided previously or contemporaneously by the parent, otherwise the pre-owned assets charge will apply.

The parent could then give the purchase money away to, say, grandchildren (or even to a child if it was clear that there was no prior agreement to do so) and benefit from one or other of the lifetime gift exemptions, from using an unused portion of the nil-rate band, or hope to survive for at least three years so as to benefit from taper relief. There can be no prior arrangement to make gifts from the purchase price, otherwise the associated operations rules will apply to negate any tax benefit. Neither can any part of the price be left outstanding on loan unless the terms are such that a commercial lender would require. After the purchase the property will no longer have the benefit of the principal private residence capital gains tax exemption and as usual, the cost of the legal fees and disbursements such as stamp duty land tax must be weighed against inheritance tax savings.

Discretionary trusts
A taxpayer might consider creating a discretionary trust in respect of part or the entirety of his share of the family home in his will and this is discussed in the following chapter.

Non-financial risks and dangers
In addition to any fiscal risks of a scheme involving the family home failing there can be other dangers and problems. Consider, for example, the case of a parent who wishes to give or sell a share of the family home to a daughter. After the gift the parent and the daughter would both own and be entitled to use the house. This might not be a good idea, especially if a daughter were to:

◆ give her share of the house away in the joint lifetimes of the parent and the daughter, or

◆ marry, or

◆ predecease the parent married but intestate or with a will which left her estate to the daughter's husband/partner who remarried, or to any third party, or

◆ become bankrupt.

Apart from any question of problems that might arise from sharing the use of the home, the new part-owner might wish to cash in the share of the house and attempt to force a sale. While a parent may justifiably think he can rely upon his daughter not attempting to force a sale, can he rely upon her future husband who he may not even have met or her trustee in bankruptcy?

What would happen if after making the gift the parent decided that he wished to move elsewhere? Would this necessitate a sale of the property, perhaps against the co-owner's wishes? Would the parent's share of the net proceeds of the sale and any other funds he had be sufficient for him to acquire another property?

A lifetime gift of a share of the family home to a child who lives with the parent can create particular problems if the donor has several children, all of whom he wishes to benefit equally and he intends to compensate the others by bequests in his will. When considering the provision to be made in the will, account will have to be taken of the fact that neither the size of the estate at the unpredictable date of death nor the variation in the value of the share in the house between the date of the gift and that date can be calculated in advance with any certainty. Furthermore, if the parent does not survive the making of the gift by seven years, the lifetime gift will swallow up most, if not all, of the nil-rate band with the result that the effective tax rate on the death estate and the bequests made by the will will be higher than that on the lifetime gift of the share of the house.

A factor which sometimes influences a taxpayer to give away his home during his lifetime is liability to contribute to possible future residential or nursing home fees. Readers should be aware that gifts made with the intention of depriving a taxpayer of assets which would otherwise be included in the value of assets used to determine his liability to pay or contribute to residential home fees can be ignored by a local authority and the local authority will pursue the donee with a view to including the gifts in the assessable assets and if necessary claiming them.

Conclusion

Any scheme to reduce inheritance tax involving the family home which fails can result in disastrous consequences all round: there will be no saving of inheritance tax, in many cases an income tax liability under the pre-owned assets charge will arise and unless the recipients of the home occupy it as their principal private residence, any gain that they make when they dispose of the property will be taken into account when assessing their liability to capital gains tax.

In my opinion it is advisable for a taxpayer to attempt to keep a roof over his head irrespective of the effect it will have on the inheritance tax payable on his death or home fees payable during his lifetime. Too often has a child whose business is in financial difficulties decided that it would be better for an elderly parent to pass the family home to him to avoid inheritance tax on the parent's death or future home fees and incidentally allow him to use it as collateral security for the failing business. It is not worth taking the risk that you or your spouse or civil partner could be made homeless merely to save inheritance tax or home fees and anyone who is reasonably able to care for himself should be given independence and security by retaining the family home rather than having to rely upon the goodwill of the family.

PENSION SCHEME BENEFITS

Most pension schemes provide death-in-service benefits which are payable to beneficiaries chosen at the discretion of the scheme's trustees. The trustees will normally take into account the wishes of the scheme member who can write to the trustees or fill in a letter of request expressing his wishes. The member should request that the benefits are not paid into his estate but paid directly to specified persons so that they do not swell his taxable estate.

USING ANNUITIES AND TRUSTS OF LIFE POLICIES

If a reasonably large sum is surplus to the taxpayer's likely requirements it might be a good idea for the taxpayer to purchase an annuity and use the annuity to fund the premiums on a whole life policy on his life written in trust for intended beneficiaries. The premiums would probably be exempt under the gift exemptions for normal gifts out of income or the annual or small gifts allowances and the policy proceeds, being written on trust for the intended beneficiaries, would be outside the taxpayer's taxable estate.

The scheme will only work to save inheritance tax if it can be shown that the purchase of the annuity and the effecting of the life policy are not 'associated operations'. Associated operations, as defined in section 268(1) of the Inheritance Tax Act 1984 in this context are, in essence, two or more operations or transactions 'one of which is effected with reference to the other, or with a view to enabling the other to be effected or facilitating its being effected ... whether those operations are effected by the same persons or different persons and whether or not they are simultaneous'. It is therefore more likely that it will be possible to save inheritance tax in this way if the annuity and the life policy are purchased from different companies and it almost always pays to shop around to obtain the best value at the relevant time. Such a scheme would have to be carefully checked out in the light of the individual taxpayer's particular circumstances including his income tax position and the rates available at the relevant time to see if it is likely to prove worthwhile. The life policy should be one with fixed premiums. Once entered into there is no going back upon such a scheme. It must also be remembered that the trust of the life policy will be a relevant property trust subject to the ten-year periodic and exit charges unless it qualifies as a trust for the disabled.

EQUALISING ESTATES BETWEEN PARTNERS OTHER THAN SPOUSES AND CIVIL PARTNERS

For parties to a happy and stable relationship, an effective way of reducing inheritance tax is to share their respective taxable wealth with a view to enabling each to make full use of their individual lifetime gift exemptions and nil-rate band in favour of others. This can be important for partners of different sex who have children but have not married and same sex partners who have adopted children but have not entered into a civil partnership, if one partner does not have assets in excess of the nil-rate band, but the other is wealthier and can afford to make some provision for the children without impoverishing the surviving partner on the wealthier partner's death. However, transfer of assets other than cash between them might incur stamp duty or capital gains tax and inheritance tax if the donor partner does not survive for seven years and the gift causes his nil-rate band to be exceeded.

DISCLAIMING AND VARYING INHERITANCES BY DEEDS OF FAMILY ARRANGEMENT

What Deeds of Family Arrangement are and how they work

It is sometimes possible for anyone who receives an unwanted inheritance to change the situation to make it more tax efficient or appropriate to the needs of all concerned. This is done by all who are affected by the inheritance entering into either a document called a deed of variation or a document called a deed of disclaimer, both of which are sometimes referred to as a Deed of Family Arrangement. If this is done within two years of the death and the statutory requirements adhered to, the variation or disclaimer can be considered for inheritance tax purposes as having been made by the deceased on his death and will not be a transfer of value by the person who gives up or surrenders the inheritance. For income tax purposes, the deeds are not retrospective to the date of death, and income which is distributed between the date of the death and the date of the deed will be taxed as that of the original beneficiary. Deeds of Family Arrangement can be used to vary inheritance rights that are given by a will or which arise on intestacy and in spite of their name need not be by deed as long as they are made in writing.

The change in the situation is effected by the beneficiary disclaiming the inheritance or by all concerned agreeing in the deed to vary the dispositions of the estate. If one of the parties concerned has died, provided all who benefit under his will or intestacy consent, his personal representatives can enter into the deed on his behalf. If minors or others who do not have full legal capacity are involved it is necessary to make an application to a court to approve the rearrangement on their behalf but the court will only give its approval if it considers that the rearrangement is for the benefit of the minor or other person who is lacking full legal capacity.

The difference between a disclaimer and a variation

The difference between disclaiming something inherited from a will or under the laws of intestacy and varying the provisions of a will or the laws of intestacy must be clearly understood.

To disclaim a benefit under a will or an entitlement under an intestacy is to refuse to accept it and although a disclaimer can be retracted, it can only be retracted if no other person has relied upon it to his detriment. An inheritance can only be disclaimed if the person seeking to disclaim has not already benefited from it. The inherited benefit cannot be accepted as to part and refused as to part; it is all or nothing, although if more than one gift is made to the same beneficiary in a will or inherited on intestacy, one gift may be accepted and the other may be refused and disclaimed, provided they are clearly separate gifts.

On the other hand, to effect a variation the beneficiary first accepts the gift and then varies it so that another or others benefit, either in addition to, or to the exclusion of the original beneficiary. This point is very important because it necessarily follows that having accepted the inheritance in the case of a variation, the original beneficiary can decide its further devolution and who is to benefit from it, but having refused the inheritance in the case of a disclaimer he has no further control over it and it must devolve according to the other provisions of the will or the laws of intestacy as the case may be. Although it is possible to effect a variation of the devolution of jointly owned property which is inherited as the result of being a surviving joint tenant, it is not possible to disclaim survivorship rights.

There are different inheritance, capital gains and income tax consequences that result from the difference in the nature of a disclaimer and a variation and before making a decision it is essential that specialist tax advice be sought.

If an asset has been redirected once to a different beneficiary by a deed of variation, it is not permissible to redirect it a second time, but more than one deed of variation can be entered into in respect of an estate as long as they relate to different assets.

Redirection of assets is not always a sure-fire way to protect them from claims by the trustee of a bankrupt beneficiary.

Making the deed tax effective

If the deed is to be effective for tax purposes and the Revenue is to consider the change as having been made by the deceased so that there is to be a saving of inheritance and/or capital gains tax, the following conditions must be complied with.

- The change must be made in writing and in the case of a variation all the parties affected must be parties to the document to show they consent to the changes; but in the case of a disclaimer, only the person making the disclaimer is necessarily a party to the document.

- The disclaimer or variation must be made within two years of the death.

- The document that makes the variation must contain a

statement made by all parties to it as to whether they intend it to have effect for the purposes of inheritance tax and/or capital gains tax. If they do so intend it will take effect for the chosen purpose(s) as if any variation had been made by the deceased, or as the case may be, any disclaimed benefit had not been conferred by the will or the intestacy laws.

If the variation results in more tax becoming payable, the personal representatives must be parties to the document unless, in that capacity, they hold no or insufficient funds to pay the additional tax. If additional tax is payable a fine can be imposed upon all parties to the document unless a copy of the document and a note of the additional tax payable is supplied to the Revenue within six months of the date of the document.

There is no necessity for a disclaimer to state that it is intended to take effect from the date of death; it does so automatically.

The effect of the deed

In the case of any estate where the residue is either partially or wholly exempt from inheritance tax, it is necessary to carefully consider whether any proposed disclaimer or variation will cause the total value of the non-exempt gifts to exceed the nil-rate band as a result of the grossing-up rules which are explained on page 28.

Some changes to the provisions of a will or to the devolution of an estate under the laws of intestacy can save very considerable amounts of tax if the estate is large, but others increase the amount of tax payable. The changes can affect not only inheritance tax, but also capital gains tax, income tax and means-tested social security benefit payments and may cost not insignificant legal fees to implement, but in the right circumstances and if carefully and knowledgeably done, they can be very worthwhile. The formalities for tax-effective Deeds of Family Arrangement have to be strictly observed and it is essential that advice should be taken from a solicitor or accountant who is knowledgeable about tax law before such a course of action is finally embarked upon.

It is not possible to disclaim an inheritance which is expected from the estate of someone who has not yet died.

CHOOSING INVESTMENTS

The type of investments held at death can make a considerable difference to the amount of inheritance payable because of the various reliefs (such as business relief and agricultural relief) which may be available. However, it must also be remembered that the type of investment chosen during one's lifetime can also make a vast difference to one's wealth at the time of death and investments should be chosen on their merits as investments and never be chosen solely with a view to obtaining any form of tax relief. The investments which attract the most tax relief are usually those with the greatest risk and the amount lost by market fluctuations is sometimes greater than the tax saved.

MAKING A WILL

An effective step that can be taken in life to reduce or avoid inheritance tax on death is to make a tax-efficient will. A good will will not only protect the testator's loved ones after his death and ensure that his estate goes to the people he wishes to benefit from the efforts he has made during his life; it will ensure that there is more estate to go to them. If you have persevered so far, read on.

9

Reducing Inheritance Tax by Making Your Will

When making a will and considering inheritance tax-saving possibilities, it comes as a great relief to realise that the complexities of gifts with a reservation and pre-owned assets can be ignored; they are only concerned with dispositions which take effect during the donor's lifetime.

USING EXEMPT GIFTS

Several of the types of gift which are mentioned in Chapter 1 as exempt from inheritance tax if made during the taxpayer's lifetime are also exempt if made by will, notably:

- gifts to registered charities for their charitable purposes
- gifts for national purposes including gifts to most museums and art galleries
- gifts to some political parties
- gifts of land to housing associations
- gifts the value of which does not exceed the unused nil-rate band
- gifts to a spouse or registered civil partner.

Leaving any of these gifts by will reduces the inheritance tax which would otherwise be payable.

THE IMPORTANCE OF THE NIL-RATE INHERITANCE TAX BAND

Although a taxpayer could leave his entire estate to a spouse or registered civil partner without paying any inheritance tax on death, doing so might well have compounded the problem when the spouse or partner subsequently died, in that what the taxpayer left and the survivor did not give away more than seven years before the survivor's death or did not spend before death, was added to the assets the survivor already held in his name and in some cases to the assets of a trust under which the survivor had a right to benefit during his lifetime and might thus cause the survivor's estate to exceed the nil-rate band and incur 40% tax.

On the other hand if a taxpayer was only moderately well off, the surviving spouse or civil partner needed the family home and other assets to live reasonably comfortably after the first death and assets could not easily be given to others to make full use of the nil-rate band. There were too many beneficiaries and not enough estate! It was important to make use of the nil-rate inheritance tax band. At present rates and allowances up to £120,000 more inheritance tax can be incurred if the nil-rate band is not used and before the Pre-Budget Proposals of 2007 this dichotomy was solved to some extent by making use of a nil-rate band discretionary will trust of which the spouse or civil partner was one of the potential beneficiaries and leaving the remainder of the estate to the spouse or partner.

If, as anticipated, the Pre-Budget Proposals of October 2007 are enacted in the 2008 Finance Act and they become law, the use of the nil-rate band discretionary will trusts described in the later section of this chapter will, in most cases fall out of use and they will be replaced by claiming transferability of the nil-rate band. However, for some time yet many will continue to exist and in special circumstances and for reasons other than inheritance tax, they will continue to have some uses. For these reasons a discussion of them is included in this book.

USING NIL-RATE BAND DISCRETIONARY TRUSTS

WARNING

No one should contemplate setting up or managing a trust without assistance from a lawyer who has considerable expertise in trusts and taxation. Trusts and the taxation of trusts are very technical subjects and the law and practice of trusts and taxation are in a state of constant evolution.

The basics of a nil-rate band discretionary will trust scheme

As explained in Chapter 7 a discretionary trust is a trust in which the trustees of the trust are given discretion as to how the capital and/or income of the trust is to be shared between the various potential beneficiaries of the trust. Although it is usual to leave a letter or note to inform the trustees how the settlor wishes the trustees to exercise the discretion they have been given, the settlor's wishes should not be included in the document which creates the trust and the trustees must be legally free to ignore them, although they will usually feel under a moral duty to carry them out. If the trust is to have the benefits of a discretionary trust and not be considered by the Revenue to be an interest in possession trust, the potential beneficiaries must be given no right or entitlement to benefit from the trust unless and until the trustees decide to make an allocation to them from the trust funds; until that time they have only the hope of benefiting.

The basics of a nil-rate band discretionary will trust scheme are that a discretionary trust is set up in the will of a married person or a civil partner to the value of the testator's unused nil-rate band and the testator's other assets are left to the testator's spouse or civil partner. On the testator's death the assets left to the trust are exempt from inheritance tax because they do not exceed the testator's previously unused nil-rate band and the remainder of the estate escapes inheritance tax under the surviving civil partner/spouse exemption.

The potential beneficiaries of the trust include the survivor, who is frequently appointed to be one of the trustees. The intention is that the surviving spouse/civil partner shall benefit from the trust funds or the income they produce from time to time during her lifetime, as far as is considered necessary or desirable. It is therefore possible that the survivor will have the benefit of the entirety of the testator's estate and be in no worse a position than she would have been if the assets had been left to her directly but there is, and necessarily should be, no guarantee, because it is the essence of a discretionary trust that the allocation of the trust funds and their income shall be in the discretion of the trustees and no one shall have a **right** to benefit from them unless the trustees make a decision to that effect.

If the first spouse/partner to die leaves sufficient liquid assets such as cash or investments they are transferred to the trustees and then the trustees are able to exercise their discretion to make such payments as the trustees think fit to the survivor. The survivor inherits the residue of the estate including the deceased's share of the family home if it was jointly owned. There is no problem: the survivor has the security of ownership of the entirety of the family home, there is a reduction in the inheritance tax that would have been payable on the second death and the survivor has the possibility of benefiting from the estate to the extent that she would have benefited from it if it had been left directly to her.

Using the family home in a nil-rate band legacy discretionary will trust scheme

Tenancies in common and joint tenancies
If the first spouse/partner to die leaves insufficient liquid assets (such as cash or investments) to use to pay the nil-rate band legacy and the survivor wishes to continue to live in the family home, the survivor and the trustees of the discretionary trust resort to using one of the debt/charge or loan discretionary trust schemes referred to in the following sections of this chapter.

If the family home is jointly owned and it is intended to use the testator's share of the family home in a discretionary trust schemes the co-owners must own the home as tenants in common and not as joint tenants because property owned as joint tenants passes on death to the survivor notwithstanding any provision to the contrary in the deceased's will. If the home is owned as joint tenants the co-ownership joint tenancy must first be converted into a tenancy in common by severing it. Severance of a beneficial joint tenancy is a simple transaction that must be carried out before death and not by will, but it can be easily and cheaply carried out as explained below, without the assistance of a solicitor.

How do you know whether jointly owned property is held as joint tenants or tenants in common? As a first step the wording of the title documents should be considered. Married couples and civil partners usually, but not necessarily, own their homes as joint tenants. If there is any evidence to show that joint owners own separate shares of the property as opposed to each joint owner owning the entirety, the joint ownership is a case of tenancies in common. Joint tenants always own property equally and words or actions indicating that the joint owners own unequally always means that the assets are held as tenants in common.

Conversion of a joint tenancy into a tenancy in common by severing it can be achieved by one joint tenant merely writing and signing a note to the other(s) informing the other(s) that the joint tenant is severing the joint tenancy by the note 'I give you notice that I hereby sever the joint tenancy which exists between us in the property known as...' will suffice. The note should be handed to the other co-owner(s) and it is a wise precaution to arrange for the other co-owner(s) to sign a receipt (which can be written on the note) to confirm that they have received the document and to place the receipted copy of the document with the title documents. If the property has a title which is registered at HM Land Registry, the receipted copy should be sent to the Land Registry at the District Land Registry (the address of which can be found noted on the official copy of the Land Registry title information document) for noting in the Registry's records. When communicating with the Land Registry always quote the Land Registry Title Number, which appears in the copy of the Land Registry title information document.

It is possible for a joint tenant to sever the joint tenancy and create a tenancy in common by other conduct showing an intention to do so, but such a severance is much more difficult to prove.

The debt/charge discretionary will trust legacy scheme

This is a scheme which has been frequently used if the first spouse/partner to die left insufficient liquid assets (such as cash or investments) to use to pay the nil-rate band legacy, the survivor wished to continue living in the family home and the trustees did not wish to risk a large capital gains tax bill on the first to die's share of the family home when it was eventually sold.

The will setting up the trust contained a clause which authorised the trustees of the trust to accept an unsecured debt repayable on demand or a charge on assets as part or as the entirety of the trust funds. If the first spouse/partner to die left insufficient liquid assets for the house to be transferred to the survivor and assets to fulfil the legacy being transferred to the trust, the trustees exercised that power and the deceased's executors gave the trustees an IOU for the nil-rate band legacy or the deficiency or placed a charge in favour of the trust upon assets of the estate and then transferred the assets including the deceased testator's share of the family home to the survivor subject to the charge. Placing a charge on the assets is, in layman's terms, mortgaging them to the trust.

The debt or charge was paid off when the assets were sold or as and when the survivor was able to repay it or when the survivor died. If it still existed at the survivor's death the debt or charge reduced the value of the survivor's estate and consequently any inheritance tax payable in respect of the estate.

The loan scheme

A variant of the debt/charge scheme is the loan scheme, under
which assets are loaned by the trust to the survivor, who signs an
IOU for them. The loan scheme seems to differ little from the
debt/charge scheme but in the debt/charge scheme it is the
executors and not the survivor who create the charge or sign the
IOU. The loan scheme is much riskier.

Section 103 of the Finance Act 1986

The effect of section 103 of the Finance Act 1986 is that a debt or
liability cannot be deducted from the value of an estate to reduce
inheritance tax if it was incurred in return for something derived
from the creditor; or to put it another way, a person cannot give
cash or assets to another and then borrow them back and count
the indebtedness or liability as a debt against his estate for
inheritance tax purposes. Section 103 therefore prevents the debt/
charge/loan schemes from successfully reducing the tax if the
spouse/partner who dies is one who has never had assets not
derived from the survivor spouse/partner, e.g. a spouse who has
never worked and never had an inheritance.

Warnings

♦ If there is a danger that the net estate will be insufficient to
  meet the nil-rate band legacy to the trust and leave sufficient
  value for the home to be transferred to the survivor, the
  testator will need to consider carefully what he intends to
  achieve and the wording of his will. If he leaves a specific
  legacy of his unused nil-rate band to the trust and the home is
  included in the residue of his estate, the legacy will fail to be
  paid in full and residuary estate (including the home) will be
  reduced to meet the shortfall. If the survivor wishes to have the
  home transferred to him it will be necessary to make

arrangements to meet the legacy. In the same circumstances of an insufficiency, if the home is bequeathed to the survivor subject to the legacy, the legacy will be reduced as far as is necessary and the home will be unaffected.

◆ Nil-rate band discretionary will trust legacy schemes only work if there is a valid marriage or registered civil partnership; there is no such thing in English law as a 'common law wife' or a 'common law husband' and the survivor exemption from inheritance tax does not apply in the cases of different-sex partners who are not legally married or same-sex partners who have not registered their partnership.

◆ A nil-rate band discretionary trust will only be effective in reducing inheritance tax if it can be seen to be a genuine discretionary trust and not a sham simply aimed at avoiding tax. If both the settlor and the trustees have the common intention that the trustees will deal with the trust assets in accordance with the wishes of the settlor, the law will consider the trust to be a sham. If only the settlor has that intention, the trust will not be considered to be a sham. To show that the trust is not a sham and that the trustees are genuinely exercising independent discretion, the trustees should hold regular meetings, minutes should be taken and kept, the trust's investments should be monitored, accounts kept, income tax returns made and the needs of each potential beneficiary should be considered and resolutions passed. Not all the income of the trust should be paid to the survivor and it certainly should not be paid by regular payments or a bank mandate. A near cash reserve (a reserve that can be easily and quickly converted into cash) should be maintained to meet tax and administrative expenses and if necessary part of the loan should be recalled to meet them. The debt or loan can be structured to be index linked or bear interest. Every effort should be made to show that the trust is not merely a gift to the survivor, in which case it would form part of the survivor's estate and be taxable when he or she died.

◆ Finally I repeat that anyone contemplating a discretionary trust must employ an expert to prepare and advise upon the trust. Remember that, as is the case with most tax-avoidance schemes, they are complicated, expensive if they go wrong and they are often difficult or impossible to unscramble if the law changes. If a government feels that too much tax is being lost it might decide to clamp down on the trusts and even introduce retrospective legislation to do so.

Taxation of nil-rate band discretionary will trusts

Tax is charged on the estate of the person whose will sets up the trust, at his death, in the usual manner allowing for the nil charge for any unused nil-rate band. As is usual with discretionary trusts, the trust funds might suffer an inheritance tax charge every ten years if they exceed the nil-rate band at that date. The current maximum rate for the charge is 6%. The tax is also charged upon capital paid out of the trust at the same maximum rate but there is no inheritance tax payable on capital paid out of the trust in the first ten years because in that period the tax rate is calculated upon the value of the trust at the date of the death which by definition did not exceed the nil-rate band. Neither is tax payable on the death of a potential beneficiary unless the trust terminates on the death, because the trust funds belong to the trust and do not belong to or form part of the estate of any potential beneficiary. No potential beneficiary has any entitlement until the trustees make an allocation to him.

Nil-rate band legacies without a discretionary trust

Married couples and civil partners can save inheritance tax by making use of each testator's nil-rate band by leaving a legacy equivalent to the value of the unused nil-rate band to others and the residue of the estate to the surviving spouse/partner/charity without the necessity of a discretionary trust if they wish, but by not using a nil-rate band discretionary trust they lose the flexibility which a discretionary trust gives and the surviving spouse/civil partner will not have the possibility of benefiting from the funds bequeathed by the legacy.

Similarly, the estate of a testator who has no civil partner or spouse and who leaves the residue of his estate for charitable purposes and a legacy equivalent to the balance of his unused nil-rate band will suffer no inheritance tax.

The advantages of using a nil-rate band discretionary will trust scheme

The main advantage of using a discretionary trust, instead of a straight legacy, is flexibility. The trustees' powers can be used to meet differing circumstances which arise from time to time and circumstances which cannot be foreseen at the time the trust was created.

If the spouse or registered civil partner is included as a potential beneficiary of the trust, the trustees will be able to allocate so much of the income and capital of the trust to her as is appropriate having regard to her needs, the size of the residue she inherits, her tax position and any social security benefits and entitlement limits.

The taxpayer's spouse/civil partner can be appointed as a trustee and if the will includes her among the potential beneficiaries of the trust, the trustees can make income and capital payments in her favour and she need be little worse off than if the entire estate had been left to her. At the same time the trustees are able to consider and meet the needs of the other potential beneficiaries. Because the trust is discretionary and the funds belong to the trust and not to the survivor, they will not be taken into account for any means-tested benefits the surviving spouse/partner might make.

The costs of setting up and administering a discretionary trust are substantial and in spite of the savings that can be made by using them, as a result of the proposals contained in the 2007 Pre-budget Review described in the next section, they are likely to be superseded after 9 October 2007 by the use of the transferable nil-rate band.

USING THE TRANSFERABLE NIL-RATE BAND

The 2007 Pre-Budget Review proposals

In the 2007 Pre-Budget Review, the Chancellor of the Exchequer announced that in respect of deaths on or after 9 October 2007, the inheritance tax nil-rate band of a married person that remained unused on a spouse's death would be transferable to his surviving spouse upon her subsequent death, no matter when the first person died and the same would apply in the case of registered civil partners. Transferability is limited to those who are legally married and to civil partners and is not available to others who inherit e.g. to different sex partners who are not legally married or to same sex partners who have not registered a civil partnership or between parent and child and transferability is lost if the marriage or partnership is dissolved before the second death. Neither is transferability available on any other occasion but death; it is therefore not available when the survivor makes an immediately chargeable lifetime gift, but it is available against additional tax payable on the survivor's death in respect of the gift if the survivor dies within seven years of making the gift.

The transfer of the unused nil-rate band can only be claimed if the second death takes place on or after 9 October 2007; it is not claimable if both of the spouses or both of the civil partners died before that date.

If a taxpayer has had more than one previous marriage or civil partnership that ended in death, the unused nil-rate bands of all of the previous spouses or partners can be transferred up to a maximum transferable amount equal to 100% of the nil-rate band at the date of the second death. The unused nil-rate band available on the death of the survivor is increased by the proportion of the nil-rate band that remained unused immediately after the previous death, for example, if the earlier death took place in June 2002 and involved a taxable estate of £125,000 when the nil-rate band was £250,000, 50% of the nil-rate band was unused on the first death and if the second death takes place in May 2007, when the nil-rate band is £300,000, it will be possible to claim an increase of 50% of the 2007/8 nil-rate band on the second death to increase the 2007 death nil-rate band from £300,000 to £450,000. It is the mathematical proportion of the unused nil-rate band which is transferable, not the unused cash sum.

If the entire estate is left to a surviving spouse or a civil partner under an arrangement effected by a tax compliant two-year discretionary trust as explained later or presumably under a tax compliant deed of family arrangement, none of the previously unused nil-rate band will be used and 100% will be transferable.

Inheritance tax replaced capital transfer tax which had itself replaced estate duty. If a spouse or civil partner dies after 9 October 2007 and his or her spouse predeceased and died under the rules relating to capital transfer tax or estate duty, any unused allowances of the predeceasing spouse or civil partner may be used to increase the nil-rate band of the surviving partner. These allowances will not include a surviving spouse exemption and will be based on the basic individual allowances for deaths before 21 March 1972 when for the first time under the estate duty system a £15,000 surviving spouse exemption was introduced. In respect of deaths under the capital transfer system which was introduced on 13 March 1975, the surviving spouse and nil-rate band provisions apply in the same way as they apply for inheritance tax.

The law did not provide for registered civil partnerships before 5 December 2005 and consequently there was no surviving civil partner's allowance before that date.

How to claim
The claim to transfer must be made on the prescribed Inland Revenue form which is downloadable from H. M. Inland Revenue and Customs website and it must be made within 24 months of the month in which the last death took place. The claim must be supported by a large amount of factual information and documentation concerning the earlier death and the estate and will

not be agreed on the first death. It is therefore wise to retain the entire probate files relating to the first death until the second death and for those who will be the personal representatives of the second to die to be made aware of where files may be found.

The effect of the proposals

The Inland Revenue is presently acting in accordance with the Pre-Budget Report proposals and if, as anticipated, the transferability proposals are enacted unchanged in the Finance Act 2008, there will be fewer estates liable to inheritance tax. Schemes using nil-rate band discretionary trusts or equalisation of estates between spouses and between civil partners to reduce inheritance tax will become largely irrelevant in most situations because it will be possible to achieve the same inheritance tax results by claiming transferability of the unused nil-rate band, but equalisation of estates will continue to be used

- to minimise the assets that will be available when calculating nursing or residential home fees

- if there is a real fear of a future government imposing a wealth tax.

Choosing from the available post 9 October 2007 routes

After the 2007 Pre-Budget Review there are three possible routes from which a choice can be made:

- use a nil rate band discretionary trust or

- give the value of the nil-rate band directly to the beneficiary (in which case the surviving spouse or civil partner will not benefit from it) or

◆ transfer the assets to the survivor so that the unused nil-rate band can be used on the second death.

Nil-rate-band discretionary trusts might still be useful if made during the taxpayer's life:

◆ to minimise the assets that will be available when calculating nursing or residential home fees

◆ if there is a real fear of a future government imposing a wealth tax

or by the taxpayer's will if the taxpayer is undecided and wishes to retain some flexibility and have a second bite at the asset allocation cake through his trustees. In appropriate circumstances the trustees can still give the survivor the benefit of the nil-rate band by exercising their discretion and making an outright transfer to her and the unused nil-rate band will then be available on her subsequent death.

The taxpayer might choose to make a gift of the value of the nil-rate band directly to the beneficiary rather than allow his surviving spouse's or civil partner's estate to benefit from it or to create a discretionary trust if

◆ he wishes to have certainty, for example if he is in a second marriage and wishes to be the certainty that the children of his first marriage will benefit or

◆ he can give the legacy in assets which he believes will increase in value quicker than anticipated nil-rate bands.

The taxpayer might choose to transfer the assets to the surviving spouse or civil partner so that the unused nil-rate band can be used on the second death because:

◆ to do so will enable the spouse or partner to have the use of the assets without the expense and labour involved in running a discretionary trust

◆ the traditional increases in the nil-rate band means that the unused nil-rate band is likely to be worth more in cash terms at the time of the second death than at the date of the first death because the transferable amount is the same proportion of the nil-rate band on the second death as the unused nil-rate band on the first death bears to the full nil-rate band at the time of the first death. To put the point another way if, for example, 40% of the nil-rate band appertaining at the date of the first death is unused, that figure in cash terms is less than 40% of the increased nil-rate band applicable at the time of the second death.

If the taxpayer really wishes his spouse to benefit from the entirety of his estate but he has made a nil-rate band will trust purely to save inheritance tax and in the hope that the trustees will use the trust to benefit his spouse or civil partner after his death but during her life, if he has left an outright nil-rate band legacy in favour of others for the same reason, he should now revise the will to leave his assets directly to his spouse or partner. To do so will mean that she will have the certainty of inheriting without, in the one case, the necessity of relying upon the trustees discretion and in the other case, relying upon a deed of family arrangement to which the alternative beneficiaries might not agree.

Even after the 2007 Pre-Budget Review it is still worth making lifetime gifts in appropriate circumstances because if they qualify as PETs the donor might survive long enough for them to drop out of the remaining nil-rate band calculation or to benefit from some taper relief and if they are immediately chargeable gifts they will suffer tax at only 50% of the death rate they would suffer if the nil-rate band is exceeded.

USING A TWO-YEAR DISCRETIONARY WILL TRUST

Because the taxpayer cannot foretell the precise date of his death, he cannot know what the financial position of the individual members of his family will be at that date or indeed which of his family members or friends will survive him. Neither can he know how much of his nil-rate band will have been used up by the gifts he has made or what the value of his estate or tax rates will be at that date. It is possible to overcome these problems by creating what is commonly known as a two-year discretionary trust in his will.

To create such a trust, the testator leaves his estate to his executors upon trust, with power for them to allocate it within three months and two years of the testator's death in such a manner as they see fit between certain specified beneficiaries and with a long-stop provision for the devolution of the estate if the executors fail to make an allocation within that period. It is usual to leave a letter with the will to explain to the executors the principles he wishes them to use in exercising the discretion he has given to them. The letter should make it clear that it is not binding upon the executors.

If the executors make their decision between three months and two years following the testator's death, inheritance tax in relation to the estate will be calculated as though their decision had been contained in the testator's will. A two-year discretionary trust can be a very efficient tax-saving tool and useful for a testator who has good executors and is apt to be tardy in reviewing his will. It should not be confused with a nil-rate band discretionary will trust.

USING THE INHERITANCE TAX RELIEFS

It is a waste of an inheritance tax relief such as business property relief or agricultural property relief to leave an asset that attracts the relief to exempt beneficiaries such as a spouse or civil partner, unless that beneficiary intends to give or bequeath the asset to a non-exempt beneficiary in the future. It is better to specifically bequeath the asset to chargeable people or create a discretionary trust of which chargeable people are potential beneficiaries by the will and place the asset into the trust so that the relief is used. If the asset is eligible for 100% relief the bequest can be made without adverse inheritance tax consequences and in addition to any unused nil-rate band.

The asset should be bequeathed as a specific gift and not included in a share of residue. If the asset is specifically bequeathed it will have the full benefit of the relief; if it is left as a share of residue the relief will be apportioned between all the assets of the estate. If an asset is appropriated by personal representatives in satisfaction of a share of residue or a cash legacy, it will not be considered to have been specifically bequeathed and the bequest will not attract the full relief, only its apportioned proportion. If it is desired that an asset which has not been specifically bequeathed and forms part of the residue of the estate shall achieve the status of a specific bequest after death, all parties concerned should consider a Deed of Family Arrangement.

If the spouse/civil partner wishes to have the relievable asset the testator can consider leaving it to chargeable beneficiaries (so that his estate will benefit from the relief) but on terms that the spouse/civil partner shall have an option to purchase it. Stamp Duty, Land Tax and Land Registry Fees would be payable on the purchase but they are likely to be much less than the inheritance tax saved.

It is usually better to leave relievable assets to those able to qualify for the relief in the future and should they not be chargeable persons, the asset can be left to chargeable beneficiaries so that the estate is relieved and the exempt person can possibly be left a compensating legacy or share of residue to enable her to purchase the asset from the original beneficiary.

CALCULATING THE NIL-RATE BAND: SPECIAL RULES WHEN EXEMPT BENEFICIARIES ARE INVOLVED

The grossing up of legacies

Grossing up applies to some bequests made by will. If a will does not state that any tax payable in respect of a bequest is to be paid out of the bequest, i.e. that the bequest is subject to tax, then unless the property is jointly owned or foreign property, any tax payable will be payable out of the residue of the estate. In these circumstances, if a testator leaves the residue of his estate to an exempt beneficiary such as his spouse, his registered civil partner or a registered charity, the law directs that, when calculating the inheritance tax payable in respect of the estate, for inheritance tax purposes any legacies given free of tax shall be 'grossed up', i.e. treated as a legacy of the stated sum and in addition the relevant amount of tax. If a taxpayer does not remember this point, i.e.

that any non-exempt legacy given free of tax is grossed up if the residue of the estate is given to an exempt beneficiary, he could inadvertently exceed the nil-rate band with the legacy and tax could be payable unnecessarily. Any non-exempt gifts made in the testator's lifetime must also be borne in mind when calculating what remains of the nil-rate band. Grossing-up tables are published by HM Revenue and Customs to help calculate the sums involved.

In deciding which beneficiaries are to suffer payable inheritance tax, testators must bear in mind section 41 of the Inheritance Tax Act 1984 which provides, in essence, that notwithstanding any provision of a will to the contrary, no exempt beneficiary shall be made to suffer the inheritance tax payable in respect of an exempt gift or exempt share of residue.

The 'related property' valuation rules

When calculating whether or not a bequest will exceed the nil-rate band it is also necessary to bear in mind whether or not the Revenue will consider the subject of the bequest to be 'related property'. Related property is property which would have an increased value if owned with other property which is owned by:

- a person's spouse or civil partner, or
- has been owned within the previous five years by a body to whom an exempt transfer could be made, e.g. a charity, and was so owned as the result of a transfer by the person or his spouse or civil partner. The subject of related property and the method of calculating its value have been explained more fully in Chapter 3.

SKIPPING A GENERATION

If a testator's children are wealthy he might wish to consider skipping a generation and instead of leaving bequests to his children, leaving the bequests to or for the benefit of his grandchildren to avoid increased inheritance tax being payable on the children's deaths. In this way the bequest is only taxed once instead of twice before the grandchildren inherit it.

To skip a generation can also have income tax advantages for the grandchildren if they inherit before they come of age. The income tax advantage arises from the fact that if capital transferred to a child by a parent earns income in excess of £100 in any tax year, the income is taxed as if it were the parent's income, but income earned by capital transferred by a grandparent is treated as the grandchild's own income, irrespective of the amount of the income and if it does not bring the grandchild's income above the grandchild's personal income tax allowance, any income tax deducted from the income can be recovered on behalf of the child.

Glossary

Absolutely Not for the benefit of any other person and free from any condition.

Assets Property or other items of value that are owned.

Beneficiary An organisation or person who actually or potentially benefits from the assets of a trust or who inherits.

Capital gains tax – The tax on financial gains made by selling, giving away or otherwise disposing of assets at a value which is higher than their value when they were acquired.

Civil partner A person who has entered into the relationship with another person of the same sex which is recognised by the Civil Partnership Act 2004 and registered that relationship in accordance with the terms of the Act.

Cohabitees Unmarried people who live together as man and wife or partners.

Contingent Dependent upon the fulfilment of a condition or the happening of an event.

Deceased Dead, the person who has died.

Deed of Family Arrangement (or deed of variation)– a document by which entitlements are rearranged or varied.

Discretionary trust A trust in respect of which the trustees of the trust are entitled to decide who, among specified potential beneficiaries, shall be entitled to benefit of some or all of the capital or income of the trust and in respect of which no person or organisation has a present entitlement.

Domicile The state or country with which a person has his closest links and in which he intends to make his permanent home.

Donee A person to whom something is given.

Donor A person who makes a gift.

Estate The entirety of the assets of a person that are beneficially owned; a person's wealth.

Executor A male person appointed by a will or codicil to carry out its provisions after the death of the person who makes it.

Executrix A female person appointed by a will or codicil to carry out its provisions after the death of the person who makes it.

Gift with a reservation A gift from which the giver continues to benefit after the gift has been made.

Immediately chargeable gift A gift made during life to a discretionary trust or to a company. Such gifts incur liability to inheritance tax at the time they are made instead of being taxed on the death of the giver.

Inheritance tax The tax payable on a transfer of value made by a gift on death or during life.

Interest in possession trust A trust in respect of which someone (technically known as the life tenant or tenant for life), has a present legal entitlement to benefit from the trust fund for his life or any other limited time (the interest in possession), after which the benefit of the fund will pass to another person.

Intestacy Death without having made a will.

Joint tenants People who jointly own assets in such a way that by law the ownership passes automatically to the survivor or survivors on the death of one of them.

Legacy A gift left by a will or by a codicil.

Legatee A beneficiary to whom a gift is made by a will or a codicil.

Life interest The right to benefit from something during life but not to dispose of it on death.

Life tenant A person who has the right to benefit from something during life or some other limited period but not to dispose of it on death.

Loan trust An arrangement under which a settlor lends money to a trust which the trust invests, the idea being that the growth in the investments will belong to the trust and not to the settlor and will therefore be outside the settlor's estate and not give rise to inheritance tax on the death of the settlor.

Minor A person who is under the age of 18 and who has consequently not reached the age of majority.

Nil-rate band The value of the part of an individual's taxable wealth which is below the value at which inheritance tax is charged.

PET (potentially exempt transfer) A transfer of value which will be exempt from inheritance tax if the giver survives the making of the gift by seven years but taxable if he does not.

Predecease To die before.

Residue or **residuary estate** That part of an estate which is left after all debts, liabilities, expenses and legacies have been paid and discharged.

Settlement An arrangement whereby assets are to be used by people successively.

Spouse The person to whom one is married.

Tenant in common Someone who owns a share of a jointly owned asset in such a way that he can deal with it separately from the remainder of the asset.

Testator A male person who makes a will.

Testatrix A female person who makes a will.

Transferee Someone to whom an asset is transferred.

Transfer of value A disposition of assets as a result of which wealth is reduced.

Transferor A person who transfers an asset.

Trust An arrangement under which someone called a trustee holds or manages assets (the trust fund) for the benefit of another person or organisation (the beneficiary) or people or organisations (the beneficiaries).

Trustee A person who is trusted to carry out or perform a duty or service or hold or manage property for the benefit of another person, organisation or purpose.

Index